Sisters

TIMECODES

A book series exploring individual movies minute by minute.

Also in the Series:

Gerry: Movies Minute by Minute, by Nicholas Rombes

BlacKkKlansman: Movies Minute by Minute, by Alex Zamalin

Twin Peaks: The Return, Part 8: Movies Minute by Minute, by Jeff Wood

Neptune Frost: Movies Minute by Minute, by Steven Shaviro

Point Break: Movies Minute by Minute, by Stephen Lee Naish

Sisters

Movies Minute by Minute

Johanna Isaacson

BLOOMSBURY ACADEMIC
NEW YORK • LONDON • OXFORD • NEW DELHI • SYDNEY

BLOOMSBURY ACADEMIC
Bloomsbury Publishing Inc, 1359 Broadway, New York, NY 10018, USA
Bloomsbury Publishing Plc, 50 Bedford Square, London, WC1B 3DP, UK
Bloomsbury Publishing Ireland, 29 Earlsfort Terrace, Dublin 2, D02 AY28, Ireland

BLOOMSBURY, BLOOMSBURY ACADEMIC and the Diana logo are trademarks of Bloomsbury Publishing Plc

First published in the United States of America 2026

Cover design: Eleanor Rose

Cover illustration © Steve De La Mare

A catalog record for this book is available from the Library of Congress.

ISBN: HB: 979-8-2163-7340-7
PB: 979-8-2163-7339-1
ePDF: 979-8-2163-7343-8
eBook: 979-8-2163-7345-2

Series: Timecodes

Typeset by Deanta Global Publishing Services, Chennai, India
Printed and bound in the United States of America

For product safety related questions contact productsafety@bloomsbury.com.

To find out more about our authors and books visit www.bloomsbury.com and sign up for our newsletters.

Many thanks go out to the Timecodes series editors, my Thursday night horror watching group, my co-editors at Horror Studies *and* Blind Field, *my colleagues and students at MJC, my "Love Boat" mutual aid crew, my collaborators on the diy horror film,* Precarious Souls, *the professors and peers who helped me through grad school in UCSC's Literature department, the Marxist Literary Group, and Red May.*

Special thanks go out to my partner, Hunter Bivens, for his gameness, collaboration, and support through this adventure.

CONTENTS

PREFACE

I first discovered *Sisters* in the late 1990s while pursuing what I refer to as my second bachelor's degree, obtained from the University of Reel Video (RIP), located in Berkeley, California. Every weekday after work I poured over the well-curated collection of VHS tapes, chatting with the friendly, knowledgeable, and extremely tolerant-of-obsessive-customers staff. In this way, I missed the nineties, or rather spent it elsewhere, immersed in 1970s cinema, gravitating to the wide, experimental, countercultural swings of what is now the old New Hollywood.

I was attracted to and repelled by these films, so many of which—*Easy Rider*, *Five Easy Pieces*, *Two-Lane Blacktop*—focused on the subjectivities and homosocial friendships of young, white, countercultural men. New Hollywood's dark anti-heroes and lack of closure warmed my spikey little punk heart. But even as I fell in love with naturalism as an antidote to the Reaganite Hollywood slickness and treacle I grew up with, New Hollywood's obsession with masculine authenticity got under my skin, as did its superficial, conventional, distracting, threatening, or invisible women characters.

Not so with the period's countercultural horror and horror-adjacent cinema. In these irreal, excessive, emotionally unhinged works, I found a home that, for all its imperfections and lacunae, I never left and honestly never want to leave. With this epiphany, I hunted for these oddly comforting films, where patriarchal violence and women's constricted roles were acknowledged as terror—the excruciating trials of puberty (*Carrie*), the ubiquitous atmosphere of sexual violence (*Ms .45*), the isolation of the nuclear family (*The Stepford Wives*), the enforced passivity of pregnancy (*Rosemary's Baby*), the straitjacket of motherhood (*Mommie Dearest*), the overall depersonalization of womanhood (*3 Women*), the delight and monstrosity of female embodiment (*Possession*).

These films featured few "strong female leads," nor strongly feminist directors, but that wasn't the point. Who knew what these films—tangles of 1960s hope, 1970s despair, auteur experiment, capital investment, creative collaboration—thought they were doing? All I knew was that these chaotic brews of countercultural surrealism, second wave feminism, gothic mystery, campy excess, and formal experimentation laid out a map (interior and exterior) I wanted to explore.

Sisters is an early example of feminist-themed countercultural horror, and without it, who knows if the rest could exist? Made between the waning of the studio system and the rise of the blockbuster; in the blurred 1970s' hangover following 1960s' revolutionary movements and counterculture; at second wave feminism's peak as well as its imminent cooptation; in De Palma's transition from experimental independent filmmaker to Hollywood funded auteur; *Sisters* is a mass of productive contradictions—Is it the film that made De Palma De Palma? Is it the most feminist film ever made? Does it mark the birth of De Palma's misogynist rampage through the 1970s and 1980s? Yes! No! Maybe!

With *Sisters*, De Palma's sixth feature film, his style becomes so recognizable that Chris Forrester claims "the director didn't become *the* Brian De Palma of *Scarface*, *Carrie*, or *Mission: Impossible* fame until *Sisters*." This was the film "in which the formerly swirling, amorphous fascinations that defined his first string of features coalesced into a generically singular, thrilling, and pointedly political whole."[1]

The famed queer film theorist Robin Wood called *Sisters* the most feminist film of the 1970s, citing its two main characters, Grace and Danielle, as representing both women's psychosexual oppression and the second-wave feminist desire for professional autonomy. In another essay, he claims *Sisters* to be "the definitive feminist horror film . . . among the most complete and rigorous analyses of women under patriarchal culture in the whole of patriarchal cinema."[2] But this reading seems at odds with the abundant accusations of misogyny and transphobia De Palma has drawn throughout his directing career. Says Chris Dumas, "*of course* De Palma is a misogynist; given the fact that . . . the majority of men of his generation are . . . I do not know how he could be expected not to be."[3]

Whatever De Palma's attitudes and intents, *Sisters* has revelatory potential for trans-inclusive, intersectional, leftist feminists. With hindsight we can, lovingly, take what second wave feminists had to say about cinema and representation with a grain of salt while luxuriating in our complex and contradictory feelings about brilliant, messy films like *Sisters*.

This book's eighty-nine vignette chapters explore *Sisters* from a leftist feminist perspective, indulging curiosity and heterodox opinions on questions as they arise—How does *Sisters* mark the transition from De Palma's earlier "Godardian" phase to his signature "Hitchcockian" style? How does this metamorphosis situate the film in relation to New Hollywood's anti-capitalist yet also often masculinist politics? How are *Sisters*' themes and formal moves both diagnostic and symptomatic of phallocentric film language catering to the male gaze? How do De Palma's formal choices, such as split screen, point-of-view, and long shots, inform the film's gendered thematic implications? How do the contributions of women both as performers and behind the scenes decenter or interrogate New Hollywood auteurism? How do the disappointments following the ebbing 1960s' social movements contribute to *Sisters*' gothic darkness? How can disability studies help us understand this film that, in the end, centers on the fate of "freaks"? How should we view the racial politics of a film that both gives us a Black protagonist and prematurely kills him off?

In what follows, we will meet Grace Collier, an intrepid investigative reporter who witnesses a murder. Derided by cops as a critic of police brutality and by her mother for abandoning her sacred duty to marry and bear children, Grace will resist the bourgeois family and the authoritarian state until the constraints of "strong female lead" fail her, as they have failed feminism, liberating only a few women, whose success is achieved on the backs of invisibilized feminized laborers.

Swerving from the coopted role of "strong female lead," Grace merges with her foil, Danielle, the femme fatale whose erotic appeal draws an unwitting, innocent man into her deadly lair, where she kills him. Once Grace meets Danielle we are submerged in endless, gothic night. Danielle—a "freak," victimized by marriage, institutionalization, ableism, schizo-consciousness, sexphobia—can never "lean in" to daylight, but, better, leans out into vengeance through her alter-ego—psychotic, murdered, conjoined twin, Dominique.

Sisters, says Robin Wood, is leftist "apocalypticism" countering slicker, less critical "reactionary horror." This apocalypticism, Wood suggests, is distinct from nihilism. Rather, "its very negation can be claimed as progressive."[4] The destructive forces in *Sisters* are not timeless and universal, but historical and social. The film's world *must* explode under the pressure of annihilating repression. The negativity of these oppositional films, says Wood, "is not recuperable into the dominant ideology, but [recognizes] that ideology's disintegration, its untenability, as all it has repressed explodes and blows it apart."[5] In other words, in the context of rising 1970s right-wing thought, narrative closure equals political betrayal, an endorsement of the world as it is. And whatever the faults of *Sisters*, tidy closure is not one of them.

That is, in De Palma's work, the refusal of conventional reason breeds revolutionary monsters, signifying the "struggle for recognition of all that our civilization represses or oppresses," as Wood puts it.[6] Rejecting the role of passive and pliant housewife, *Sisters*' two protagonists may look pretty, but their potent outsider energy rivals that of vampires and zombies. Wood goes so far as to suggest *Sisters* may be (in 1973) "the only really radical feminist film Hollywood has given us since the heyday of Dietrich and Sternberg."[7] "The monstrousness of woman's oppression under patriarchy and its appalling consequences for both sexes have never been rendered more vividly," Wood concludes, than in *Sisters*.[8]

Sisters is still discussed and praised—as in Quentin Tarantino's chapter framing the film as De Palma's "calling card," Marc Olivier's exploration of the film's central prop (a sleeper sofa) in his treatment of "household horrors," or David Greven's inclusion of *Sisters* in his general reevaluation of De Palma's gender and sexual politics—but no contemporary critic has lengthily taken up Wood's impassioned praise of this film.[9] Here, in conversation with brilliant critics I sometimes disagree with, I will indulge my intoxication with *Sisters*' feminist, countercultural themes, adventurous cinematography, inventive performances, and sheer weirdness. The Timecodes series' commitment to creative "gleaning" of films' lost minutes thankfully allows this lovingly granular exploration.

The title *Sisters* gets the ball rolling. "Sisterhood" may at first *sound* powerful, but the political use of the word "sisters" already points to 1970s feminism's failed promises. This was a period of great hope and disappointment as solidarity was eroded by deeply conditioned misogyny, stratification of women by race and class, policing and exclusion of lesbians and trans people, along with neoliberalism's reliance on low-waged "feminized labor." The hope for sisterhood that came with the sixties collective social movements sought to "transform society root and branch," says Nancy Fraser. But "the cultural changes jump-started by the second wave, salutary in themselves, have served to legitimate a structural transformation of capitalist society that runs directly counter to feminist visions of a just society."[10] Accordingly, in *Sisters*, rather than affirmative platitudes, we see isolated women haunted by nebulous pasts, evoking feminism's lost, transformative horizon.

Sisters' twins are less allies than uncanny doubles, rivals, antagonists, and objects of desire or the desire to desire. We never confirm which pair of women are our central "sisters" as we rotate through shifting configurations of Danielle/Grace, Dominique/Danielle, Grace/Dominique. Rather than the harmony and symmetry promised in the concept of twins, *Sisters* serves fragmentation alongside politically potent denaturalization, predicting our current post-feminist, tradwife-ist, Dobbs-era Gothicism. But more than a warning, *Sisters* offers monstrous redemption as our wretched Cassandra/Danielle is twinned with her potent double, the Medusan Dominique, who, we will see, seizes the master's (surgical) tools to destroy the master's house, balls, spleen, reality . . .

Minutes 1–88

Minute 1

A fetus curled in utero, blurred in its cloudy amniotic sac. The tiny, veined profile conveys vulnerability. A frontal shot of its wide-set eyes expresses demonic accusation. Credits roll over the translucent being, appearing as both biological reality and nebulous mystery. Every time we think we know what we're seeing, a rapid cut challenges our perspective.

We can't help but think of Stanley Kubrick's *2001*, which graced the screen five years before *Sisters*, in the politically and culturally volatile year of 1968. *2001*'s prominent Star Child, a fetus floating in space, suggests evolutionary consciousness, but, as Vivian Sobchack and Fredric Jameson separately insinuate, this cosmic vision belies our ideological entrapment. The fetus's portentous glazed eyes are less windows into our future dreams than distorted mirrors of our present nightmares.

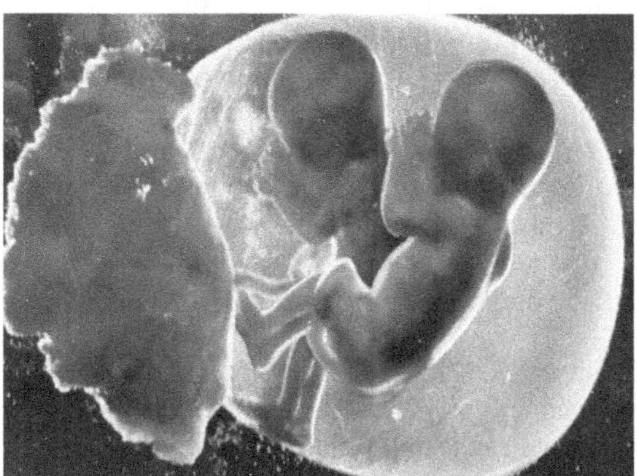

Sisters *directed by Brian de Palma © American International Pictures 1972. All rights reserved.*

Minute 2

A close-up of the fetus's mouth. Cut to waxen eyes. A sudden musical crescendo and we draw back to see *two* fully formed fetuses. Are they photographed? Are they animated? We don't know. They are alien entities rendered in an alien style, floating in space. The music cues us to feel terror at the simple *fact* of twins. A singular being generates its doppelganger. Our dreams of autonomy are blasted. The familiar is made strange.

De Palma initially planned to roll out the opening titles in silence. But when he managed to convince illustrious Hitchcock composer Bernard Herrmann to score *Sisters*, the maestro insisted that music was necessary—"No title music? Nothing horrible happens in your picture for the first half hour? You need something to scare them right away. The way you do it. They'll walk out."[1]

> To which, De Palma replied something like: "But *Psycho* . . ."
> Bernard Herrmann's retort: "YOU are not Hitchcock, for Hitchcock they will wait!"[2]
> "Herrmann was brutal," De Palma recounted, "and, of course, right."[3]

A few months later, De Palma tensely observed Herrmann in the recording studio. I'll let him take it from there:

> Herrmann raised his baton, and the orchestra sprang to attention. He looked at the large time clock overhead, counted eight beats, and jerked his baton down. The moogs wailed out and I got that same chill I'd had in the editing room a few months before. Herrmann had done it again. He was right. I couldn't leave my seat.[4]

Now, in Minute 2, enveloped by insistent, repetitive, dissonant horns, wailing Moog synthesizers, harshly plucked strings, eerily childlike glockenspiels, neither can we.

Minute 3

A gym locker room, seemingly under construction, so there is no wall between the men's and women's dressing areas. A man (Phillip) dresses as a blind woman (Danielle) enters. Accompanied by romantic, tense music she begins to reveal the curves beneath her mannish outfit. This woman stands between Phillip and us, the spectators, tempting our gazes. We can look at this blind woman, we think, with impunity.

But we are not permitted this anticipation for long, nor is our gaze rewarded with unveiled female flesh. The joke is on us as a keyhole-shaped frame closes around Phillip's face and we are made aware through wildly veering tonal and perspectival shifts that we are watching a TV audience watch Phillip and Danielle with what Abigail Lynn Coykendall describes as an "obscenely voyeuristic leer."[5] Seen through a television-shaped crop, the crass host, Ted Craft, welcomes us to "New York's newest and grooviest game," repurposing sixties-era counterculture argot to infuse life into this commercial idiocy. The point of this game show is for contestants to guess whether Phillip will "peep" as Danielle continues to unbutton her shirt.

This outright parody of the "male gaze," invisible in what Laura Mulvey calls "illusionistic narrative film," sets the tone for *Sisters*, and for De Palma's entire "red period," belying his reputation for leering misogyny. In *Sisters*, we have our cake and eat it too as cinematic pleasure both appears and deconstructs itself. Here and elsewhere, the film maps ideological visions of women's beauty and passivity, "examining patriarchy with the tools it provides . . . ."[6] As in Hitchcock's films, scopophilic eroticism is not, in this scene, a passive language, but a subject of analysis. The spectator can't claim innocence. We're not just entertained, we are made complicit. And more, we are made to *know* we are complicit.

This theme of scopophilia, emerging immediately in *Sisters*, is both homage to and commentary on Hitchcock's films. De Palma is so often regarded as derivative of Hitchcock (and so often cast his one-time wife Nancy Allen in his films) that *Saturday Night Live* once made a parody advertisement announcing, "Once a year Brian De Palma picks the bones of a dead director and gives his wife a job." Chris Dumas, though, suggests that critics misrepresent De Palma as a mere imitator of Hitchcock, when he should be seen as Hitchcock's premier interpreter, analyst, and even critic.[7]

In 1970s United States, Hitchcock was less an influence than the air directors breathed. At a certain point the twentieth century became "the Hitchcock century," Dumas claims, "a century in which [Hitchcock's] visual and narrative strategies . . . came . . . to provide the frame within which America, in some way, understood itself."[8] In this case, engagement with Hitchcock was communion with the medium itself; it's how De Palma's films conduct "an investigation of the social and technological conditions of their own possibility."[9] With Hitchcock's total imbrication with the notion of cinema itself, "it seems more appropriate to talk of symbiosis than of imitation" between the two directors, says Robin Wood.[10]

Referentiality is, after all, a key theme in both De Palma's and Hitchcock's work, making accusations of derivativeness more interesting than derogatory. In De Palma's appropriation of Hitchcock, notes David Greven, the director turns "viewing itself into the subject of filmmaking."[11] This reflexivity is more than formal; it's ideology critique. As Quentin Tarantino highlights, De Palma's adoption of Hitchcock's "Cinema First-Camera First shooting style" went against the grain of illusionistic Hollywood films, instead "call[ing] attention to the fact that the audience was watching a movie."[12]

Our perspective on De Palma's citations changes when we see him as not just a filmmaker, but a film *theorist*. The seventies were a period when the guardrails separating criticism from artistry lowered, and De Palma's intellectual curiosity, combined with his enmeshment in counterculture rebellion, allowed him to breach the divide. Dumas implies that De Palma is, perhaps, a renegade love child in an era when the towering figures of Mulvey and Hitchcock were considered the "mother" and "father" of film studies.[13] Unconsciously or consciously borrowing from both, his creations are better seen as sublation than re-creation.

Making thematic use of Hitchcock's style, De Palma wields his obtrusive camera as both spectacle and weapon. Suggests Abigail Lynn Coykendall, "De Palma successfully turns away from the individual psychopathology of the gaze . . . to beckon instead—and thereby undermine—the larger structural sociopathology that triggers . . . voyeurism."[14] That is, he guides us to reflexively explore the relation of psychology to the social. Instead of allowing the spectator to experience the magic of cinema unimpeded, De Palma blatantly inserts himself and his concerns, permitting "a critical awareness to be rediscovered in the spectator."[15] This intervention in a passive viewing experience is, for this viewer at least, a kind of freedom and release, but also a responsibility.

In Minute 3 this approach has anti-racist implications. Phillip—falsely accused of voyeurism—is himself a fetish and scapegoat for the gameshow audience's comic and sinister surveillance. De Palma places us on Phillip's side, witnessing, as Phillip soon will, these toxic gazes.

The gameshow Phillip appears on, *Peeping Toms*, is a caricature of the commodified entertainment that is the era's preferred opium of the masses. Our gaze, trained luridly on Phillip, is not simply the "male gaze," but what could be called the media-saturated spectacular gaze. Sixties-era De Palma hoped cinema could and would expose hidden truths—the imperial violence of the Vietnam War, for instance—but by the time he made *Sisters*, acknowledges Dumas, "he had come to a very different conclusion; the voyeur may become radicalized, but radicalization is always and only the first step on a path that leads inevitably to defeat."[16] *Peeping Toms*' outlandish framing not only estranges the stereotype of the bestial Black man victimizing innocent white womanhood but, as Coykendall argues, exposes "middle-America's sterile, laugh-track-guided consumption, commodification, and fetishization of the sexually and racially marked other(s)."[17]

Sisters' Peeping Toms game show is likely named after the 1960 film *Peeping Tom*, about a serial killer who records and murders his female victims with a weaponized film camera. In fact, by turning *Peeping Tom* into *Peeping Toms*, De Palma may be making a joke whose punchline is that the seemingly singular voyeur/murderer is really all of us. The ostentatious conflation of misogyny, voyeurism, and explicit-to-the-point-of-campy phallocentrism in Michael Powell's 1960 film is said to have inspired Laura Mulvey's essay "Visual Pleasure and Narrative Cinema," written in 1973 (the same year *Sisters* was released), after which feminist criticism (and film criticism in general) was changed for good. De Palma's Mulvey-esque homage to *Peeping Toms* supports Dumas's point that De Palma's work "dovetails neatly with that of psychoanalytic Film Studies, especially that which takes an explicitly feminist stance . . .."[18] Or, as Coykendall posits, if indeed De Palma's viewpoint is the "voyeuristic, masculine gaze" for which feminists have persistently criticized him, his stance is equivocal. Neither embracing nor celebrating this gaze, he instead "stimulates and interrogates" it, here and throughout *Sisters*.[19]

Back to *Peeping Toms* where we are to decide whether Phillip intends to "peep" at Danielle without her knowledge.

> **Ted Craft:** You folks there in the audience and those of you peeking in at home, Guess along with us, okay? Now, today, our peeping Tom's problem is chivalry. What does a fellow do when a pretty girl starts taking off all her clothes in front of him?

Interpellated by Ted, we merge with the all-white contestants as well as the almost all-white studio audience who sublimate their lurid desires by projecting them onto Phillip. Our laughter and "glib prurience," as Burke Hilsabeck calls it, is made impossibly grotesque when we recall the history this "bland and unanalyzed racism" has served to justify.[20] We smugly clap and wave, evoking picnickers at a lynching.

Minute 4

We see an idealized photo of the "real" Danielle, a very white woman in a very white turtleneck. She looks uncannily like Rose Armitage, *Get Out*'s innocent-appearing white liberal who will be revealed as a racist conspiring to enslave her Black boyfriend.

Cut to Phillip standing behind cage-like construction pillars. The all-white game show panel or "jury" cast a speculative verdict on what Phillip will do, uniformly predicting he will "Stop . . . Look . . . Listen." That is, Phillip will lurk and "peep" while Danielle undresses. Yet, it's us who are peeping through a keyhole, not at Danielle, but at Phillip's bewildered face.

This type of shot, argues Kenneth MacKinnon, works "to expose the sadism involved in voyeuristic activity and to castigate the normally invisible cinema audience."[21] Adds Linda Badley, De Palma's overt framing has the effect of "demonizing the white male look and refusing closure."[22] *Peeping Toms*' audience and contestants may envision themselves as Danielle's "white knights" and saviors, but we are forced to know better.

Further, we can't ignore the historical context of Phillip's vilification for gazing at a white woman. Angela Davis (who will make her way into the diegesis of this film) reminds us that white men are rarely prosecuted for rape, while this charge is disproportionately applied to Black men, whether they are guilty or not. That is, "the myth of the Black rapist" obscures actual cases of sexual violence. Rather, such accusations are used to terrorize Black communities and deter Black rebellion, while failing to protect women.[23]

Minute 4 closes with a shot of Phillip behind the locker room construction pillars, that could be jail cell bars—his vibe is more doomed prisoner than lecher at a peepshow.

Minute 5

Phillip proves himself "*Peeping Toms*' own Mr. Chivalry" by averting his gaze, rendering Pat and Fred, the white contestants betting everything on their racist assumptions, losers. Disappointed the lynching has been called off, they rally when Danielle steps onto the stage, to the studio audience's rapturous applause. The one hold-out from this spectacle is a man sitting in the front row, grimly reading a book. When the audience pan reaches him, he gazes directly at the camera, his face a caricature of opacity and menace. We will later come to know this oily man as Emil, Danielle's ex-husband, doctor, and tormentor.

Minute 6

Danielle's first words in the film: "Right now I study to be a model with Gene Fox, and also I study to be an actress."

Her charming French accent, her feminine dreams of modeling and acting, the fact that her career prospects rely on studying under a man, all introduce Danielle as a passive, compliant woman.

Phillip's first words establish him as a white-collar professional: "I'm an advertising manager for *The Amsterdam Star*."

Craft is about to confer patronizing praise on Phillip for his success when a blast of silly game show music alerts the host that there's no time left for chit-chat. The moment has come to dole out Phillip and Danielle's prizes. Danielle receives a "complete set of Reynold's stainless-steel cutlery," presumably so that she can give up her dreams of public life and act the little woman, returning to the kitchen. Worse, Phillip is granted dining and dancing for two at "Manhattan's famous African Room," a racist restaurant featuring exaggerated "tribal" masks in its advertising (unfortunately, this establishment actually existed in Manhattan at the time).

Upon receiving this "gift," Phillip's wry expression is a pinpoint of dignity, contrasting the hammy microaggressions broadcast by Ted Craft and his viewers. The camera pans once more over the audience's sea of insipid faces. The only exception to this credulous idiocy is a sole Black man, nearly hidden in a back row, grimacing at the spectacle.

Abrupt cut. Outside the claustrophobic studio, Danielle flirts with Phillip, convincing him to share his "prize" dinner and the evening with her. "I have brought my own cutlery," she jokes. This might (and perhaps should) come across ominously, but the tone here is genuinely light, emphasizing Danielle's charm.

Danielle, we learn, has an appetite. When Phillip doesn't respond to her invitation she persists: "I don't bite, you know. That is if I'm filled I don't bite." In a conventional horror movie, this desire to get "filled" would mark Danielle as a slut, and thus expendable. But *Sisters* will explore this "lack" with nuance, avoiding easy virgin/whore dichotomies.

Armond White goes so far as to link women's frequent initiation of casual sex in De Palma's films to sex-positive gender subversion and gay cruising.[24] Danielle's freedom here is echoed in De Palma's later film *Dressed to Kill*, when Kate (Angie Dickinson) pursues and has sex with a handsome stranger she wordlessly picks up in a museum. Offers David Greven: "Kate Miller's desire for sexual pleasure has little to do with male fantasy and everything to do with her own desires for pleasure, connection, and attention."[25]

A generous reader of De Palma's films, such as Linda Badley, sees these moments of women's sexual agency in line with the sex-positivity that marks contemporary, liberatory strains of feminism.[26] This is all to say that Danielle and Phillip's doomed fate is not punishment for their fling. To the contrary, the pleasure they take in each other intensifies the tragedy of their fall. In this brief moment of intimacy, we glimpse the plentitude to be enjoyed in a world Phillip and Danielle will never fully inhabit, one liberated from the constraints of racist patriarchy.

It's impossible to disentangle De Palma's patriarchal desires and fears regarding sex and women from this liberatory, sex-positive message, but it may be helpful to periodize his work in relation to the second-wave anti-porn movement, including WAP (Women Against Porn) and WAVPM (Women Against Violence in Pornography and Media). It was these feminists who denounced the sex and violence in De Palma's films, but we can't completely disentangle their protest from that of the born-again Christian revival that was, notes Marcia Pally, "making the cries of brimstone and hellfire louder, slicker, and bought from their sponsor."[27]

De Palma's criticisms of second wave, anti-porn feminism were, of course, self-serving. But the director makes an interesting case that these feminists attack porn because it's sexier and more sensationalist fare than other forms of activism, such as organizing pink-collar workers.[28] Danielle serves as an example of a woman who would be excluded by the anti-porn movement (just as they would later exclude sex workers and trans women). As a model who strips on TV, she is not, by the standards of the time, a "good" feminist. But don't such "bad girls" deserve to be protected too? Before the phrase "slut shaming" came of age, *Sisters* asks, can't women desire with impunity?

Minute 7

By way of introduction to, sigh, the African Club, the camera dollies back from a close-up of a large gorilla head "decoration," emphasizing the restaurant's malevolently exoticist setting. The mood is cemented by vaguely tribal jazz and an elephant trumpet. Far from the victim of miscegenist violation that the gameshow crowd so enjoyed imagining, Danielle is the flirtatious aggressor on this doomed date, as seen by her tipsy domination of the dinner conversation.

In this moment, she describes her reaction to an attempted sexual assault by a photographer during one of her modeling gigs. In her broken English—she is originally French Québécois—she says she had called him a "son of a bastard," recounting her bravery with slurring braggadocio. Yet, she immediately qualifies this boast, "I'm not, you know, I'm not like you American's women's liberation. I don't spend my life to hate the men."

Danielle's contradictory anecdote is left ambiguous. Are we meant to distance ourselves from feminism? Should we see Danielle's disavowal of "women's liberation" as symptomatic of the self-hating woman? Is the implied criticism here against a particularly crude American feminism emphasizing man-hating rather than fighting patriarchy? We don't know. Danielle's French syntax emphasizes this estrangement. Her askew phrasing and oblique word choices lead us to deflect and question rather than absorb the meaning of her dialogue, supporting De Palma's claim to a Brechtian style.

The lifelong radical Kidder will later, in a 2016 article she pens for the leftist magazine *CounterPunch* entitled "My Fellow Americans: We Are Fools," point to her Canadian origins as providing her critical distance from US aggression—"after the endless spit ups and boasts and rants about the greatness of American militarism . . . tonight I feel deeply Canadian."[29] This anti-imperial Canadian affiliation forms another layer to Danielle's identity that will turn out to be so complex—actress, model, divorcée, former conjoined twin, madwoman, murderer.

Minute 8

As will be revealed, Danielle has never been alone, has never been free. We will learn all the gory details in succeeding scenes, but here the couple's intimate dinner table is framed as a protected oasis where this young woman can explore her autonomy and exuberance. She's a recent immigrant to the United States and still in the honeymoon phase with her new country. Finally liberated from institutionalized confinement and marriage, she's no longer a sister, a ward, or a wife. For a moment she can embody the mythically independent, American woman. She describes herself living the dream of sovereignty, standing on top of the Empire State Building, looking down commandingly on "little cars and little people."

This spatial metaphor already reveals the hierarchy at the core of the "American Dream," yet, for a moment it feels emancipatory. "Do you like to be alone?" Phillip asks. "Sometimes I do. But not tonight," Danielle responds with drunken affection.

But don't forget, we're in a horror film. This tender moment can't last. Enter Emil, stage right.

Minute 9

Emil intrudes on Danielle and Phillip's date, claiming Danielle is his wife. "I'm not married," she protests. "I have been divorced for a year. But still he follows me." Danielle is telling the truth, but as we'll see, her connections to Emil are fantastically overdetermined. She can never be free of this man who is her doctor as well as her ex-husband and accomplice. Still, this scene deliberately leads us to view Emil as a mundane symbol of patriarchal cruelty, a possessive older husband, violently attempting to break up a date between his ex-wife and her lover.

With a waiter's help, Phillip manages to kick Emil out of the restaurant. Still "chivalrous," he offers to take Danielle home, not yet knowing how far he must go to do so, let alone that he'll never return.

Sisters *directed by Brian de Palma © American International Pictures 1972. All rights reserved.*

Minute 10

Minute 9 contains the last naturalistic moment of Phillip and Danielle's relationship. But now, in Minute 10, the pair rides a ferry to Staten Island. With the wind in their hair, birds chirping encouragement, Bernard Herrmann's score swelling and swirling, the lovers are immersed in an inhuman register of emotion. As Phillip holds the whitely draped Danielle, she dreamily laments her isolation following the loss of her sister, ensuring the couple's passionate kiss will be haunted by a mysterious third.

This romantic, vertiginous moment echoes Hitchcock's *Vertigo*, in which the protagonist Scotty nearly drowns in his passion for the mysterious Madeleine Elster—who, like Danielle, will turn out to be an ambiguous double of a woman only known through dreams, fantasy, and memory. Such sublime passion bears little relation to the casual, impish flirtation characterizing Phillip and Danielle's chemistry up until now. This is operatic, psychoanalytically inflected, blindingly intense, grand guignol love in which the two parties idealize rather than see or know each other. That is, it's the kind of love that never ends well.

At this moment we thank the cinematic gods that De Palma managed to wrest Bernard Herrmann out from semi-retirement to compose a score with emotional affects so big they can be heard from space. Herrmann was famously hard to work with and harder to please—"He was a great man. I loved him. He had a terrible temper. I hope he'll forgive me . . ."—but no one else could inflect such over-saturated romantic sublimity into this quirky film, just when it's needed.[30]

As noted, *Sisters* tends to deconstruct its own spectacular indulgences. But moments like these preserve what Linda Badley calls its "guilty pleasures" for an ambivalent female gaze.[31] Here, the simultaneous offerings of sensual indulgence and calculating analysis provide a pleasure-positive, feminist experience to those who seek it, akin to what Linda Williams identifies as ecstatic bodily excess in both horror and melodrama.[32]

Minute 11

The couple pulls up to Danielle's apartment in Staten Island. Following a brief kiss by the door, Danielle stumbles down a hallway, disrobing. Though she is engaged in a sloppy striptease, the camera doesn't linger on her body. Instead, we see her as a kind of blur, in playful, drunken motion. This moment, echoed in later De Palma sequences such as when *Dressed to Kill*'s Kate Miller (Angie Dickinson) openly pursues her desire for casual sex or *Carrie*'s Carrie White (Sissy Spacek) masturbates in a public gym shower, is another fleeting utopian gesture, but one that won't withstand the crushing patriarchal forces lined up against women's sexual and sensual liberation.

Minute 12

Cut to Phillip, looking delightedly anticipatory. However, he's *not just a subject engaged in an enthusiastic tryst; he is also the* object of an impersonal gaze. Once again, the shot, cropped by Danielle's window frame, makes us complicit, forcing us to acknowledge that we are intruders rather than welcomed guests. Says De Palma, "I'm always interested in the Brechtian approach where you make the audience aware of the form that they're watching."[33]

Perhaps sensing our prying eyes, Phillip crosses the room to close the curtains. Yet the shoe is on the other foot as he approaches another window, looks out, spots a woman across the way, framed by her own window. His unreadable gaze lingers for a moment, reminding us that scopophilia is instinctual, even in this "chivalrous" man whom we trust to look away. Things get even more complicated when Phillip next notices a much creepier peeper, Emil, Danielle's ex-husband, spying on her apartment from the front yard.

Minute 13

"Does your husband make a habit of standing guard out there?" Phillip asks Danielle as she joins him at the window. The response is that Emil is a stalker who persistently follows Danielle, insisting that they can "work it out," no matter how resolutely she asserts their marriage is over. She's "empowered" to say no, but rhetoric alone won't make the violence go away.

As a Black man living in 1970s United States, Phillip is aware that confronting Emil will be futile, and instead offers to drive away and sneak back into Danielle's apartment through the back entrance. This transformation of Phillip and Danielle's open-minded, open-hearted session of free love to a covert spy game foreshadows the racialized violence they can't and won't escape.

Minute 14

For now, the plan works. Phillip drives off and Emil leaves as well. Herrmann's signature terse ostinatos build tension. As Jordan Peele and countless Black characters in horror movies instruct us, Phillip should *get out* of this ominous situation rather than sneak in through the back door of Danielle's apartment building, which is, by the way, called "The Alexander Hamilton."

We now associate Hamilton with a poppy, progressive musical, but *Sisters* reminds us of the "founding father's" dirty little secret—despite his liberatory ideals, he still trafficked in slavery (through the back door as it were). Ignoring this omen and instead marching toward his doom, Phillip re-enters Danielle's apartment with her box of cutlery in his hands, loosening his tie as if readying himself for slaughter.

Minute 15

Danielle bares her breasts and the couple embrace. A frenzied wash of strings as Phillip inches Danielle's pink satin nightgown up her thigh. This seduction is not just a romantic spectacle but a fissure, the reopening of Danielle's previous trauma. Smooth young skin gives way to a rippling mass of keloid scar tissue. A sustained close-up of this undulating cicatrix as the couple makes love.

Minute 16

Scar tissue dissolves into a white, textured window screen. Pan down and across a white apartment—white pillows, white walls, white Danielle moaning in her white sofa bed under her white blankets. The moans aren't sexual. That part of the film is over. Now, the night terrors have begun. Danielle wakes up in a disoriented sweat.

This white terror surrounding the innocently sleeping Phillip can't be unintentional. De Palma's earlier experimental film *Hi, Mom!* was steeped in sixties-era anti-racist imagery. Observes John Ashbrook, "Whereas traditional semiotics would ascribe only good intentions to the color white, De Palma turns that on its head. Bad things happen in white houses, bad guys wear white hats. Evil is almost always enacted under the cover of white." [34]

Minute 17

Danielle stumbles to the bathroom, swallows two red pills, and sets the remaining two precariously on the sink's edge. A woman's voice calls out twice, "Danielle." This is our introduction to Dominique, Danielle's mysterious twin who, throughout *Sisters*, will remind us that a woman must be forever divided from herself: virgin/whore, helpmeet/hussy. Though we may attempt "some kind of deal with the devil to be free of [these doubles]," says Naomi Klein, "they haunt us, seeking vengeance."[35]

Minute 18

Danielle disappears into her bedroom. We hear but don't see her speaking to Dominique in French. Jake Cole sees this interaction as an example of De Palma's "sly, Brechtian technique," highlighting "the artifice of film."[36] The women's voices are similar, but we can distinguish Danielle's sweet timbre from Dominique's harsh, infuriated intonations. Clearly, Danielle was not permitted by Dominique to have sex with Phillip. Danielle, a grown woman, tells halfhearted lies met with Dominique's disbelief:

> "How could you bring him back here?"
> Danielle deflects: "I'm tired and I don't really feel well. Try to understand."

But somehow—that has to do with centuries of punishing women for any signs of active desire or sexual agency—we know that Dominique *won't* understand.

Minute 19

Exposition builds slowly and convolutedly in *Sisters*. We are often literally distanced from the plot's central action. The sisters' conversation is revelatory but remote, heard through muffled walls. Plus, they're speaking French made barely legible through white-on-white subtitles.

In an escalating argument, Dominique complains about being kept involuntarily in a hospital. Danielle responds that Dominique's institutionalization is for her own good. Dominique is furious that Danielle slept with a man, expressing disgust and moral outrage. Danielle tries to placate her sister, but it is impossible.

In his distracted eavesdropping on a conversation he can't understand, Phillip knocks Danielle's two remaining pills—stark red against the gleaming white sink—down the drain.

Minute 20

Entering the bathroom, Danielle explains Dominique is her twin sister, temporarily released from an insane asylum to celebrate their shared birthday. Phillip still has time to *get out* of this menacing situation, but his "chivalry" prevents him, evoking the punishments that historically follow when a Black man sleeps with a white woman.

Minute 21

Danielle dispatches Phillip to the pharmacy for some medication. For a moment, their two worlds diverge radically.

Danielle, confined to her white cell, lives in psychotic time, babbling submissively to Emil on the phone, looking frantically for her two missing pills. Phillip, on the other hand, escapes the cloistered apartment into his last moments of comforting quotidian time, running errands for Danielle on the streets of Staten Island.

Minute 22

Momentarily released from Danielle's claustrophobic urgency, Phillip orders an (in retrospect heartbreakingly innocent) pink and white birthday cake for the "sisters." The bakery's cake decorator hasn't arrived, so Phillip guides the saleswoman's hand, inscribing the cake with Danielle and Dominique's names. This agonizingly slow process is intercut with shots of Danielle writhing on her bathroom floor, grasping for the last of her sanity.

De Palma here chooses more traditional cross-cutting over his soon-to-be signature split screen, saving the big guns for the drama to come. Moving at a post-coitally relaxed pace, Phillip dawdles over his errands, unaware that every minute he delays contributes to Danielle's mounting, lethal hysteria.

Minute 23

When Phillip finally returns to the Alexander Hamilton apartment, he doesn't spot Emil sitting in his car, smoking. But Emil sees him, and we see him too. The shot emanates from Emil's passenger seat, so we seem to be riding along with Emil's bad intentions. We know that Danielle called her ex-husband in a panic. So why does he sit and watch rather than rush inside? As a white, male voyeur, Emil does not directly commit murder, but he is its instrument. Emil's passive gaze is complicit in what comes next, as is ours.

Minute 24

Again, Phillip enters the Alexander Hamilton from the rear entrance, seemingly relegated to errand-boy. In this vein, *Sisters*' original script emphasized the racial implications of Phillip's position. One omitted scene shows Phillip taking Danielle home from a trip to the doctor's office and getting into an argument with another driver, who calls him the N-word.[37] In another deleted scene, thuggish white guys glare at Phillip and Danielle while they kiss "and you think," De Palma says, "my god he's going to go over to Staten Island and get maimed."[38]

Some critics claim casting Phillip with a Black actor seems accidental, since his race is rarely referred to overtly. But these omitted scenes along with many other subtle moments in the plot (and some not so subtle ones such as the date scene in The African Room), underscore that casting Lisle Wilson as Phillip (De Palma's dream choice was Sidney Poitier) was an intentional, politicized choice.

Following a long walk down the aorta-like, blood-orange and yellow halls of the Alexander Hamilton, Phillip enters Danielle's antiseptically white apartment. In yet another act of servitude, he painstakingly unwraps and prepares her birthday cake. The cake serves as a narrative device to galvanize Danielle's psychotic violence, while the cake knife furnishes a weapon equally phallic and domestic. But, amid this intrigue, the music here, a "simple, sad motive" describes Steven Smith, also reminds us "of Philip's kindness and the wastefulness of his death."[39]

As Phillip finishes this task, Danielle lies passed out on the sleeper sofa, that metaphor for De Palma's unfurling themes. Emerging from her cocoon of blankets, she will be possessed by her "evil twin," Dominique.

Minute 25

In *Sisters*, De Palma is never not playing with the gaze, with gender, with race. In this buildup to the film's most violent scene we first see a "feminized" Phillip concentratedly performing a domestic task, lighting the candles on a pink, flowery cake. But then, as Phillip approaches Danielle, we cut to what looks like a killer's POV with a looming downward tilted shot of the cake, the knife closing in on an unconscious, helpless woman. Upon reaching the sofa bed, though, Phillip presents himself as a sacrifice. He kneels and hands Danielle the knife, conspicuously baring his neck in the process. In this sequence of shots, Phillip is shown as an overdetermined perpetrator and victim at once.

Sisters *directed by Brian de Palma © American International Pictures 1972. All rights reserved.*

Minute 26

But Phillip's neck is not what Danielle is after. Emerging from the blankets as a transformed, wild-eyed creature, barely recognizable as human, she thrusts the knife into his groin and then his mouth, castrating and silencing this man before our eyes. Slow-motion shots and rapid cuts estrange this climactic moment while drawing immediate comparisons to *Psycho*.

Blood spatters against a white wall. In a split diopter shot, the murderer and victim share the screen in equal proportions and focus. On the left, Danielle (or Dominique) shakes her head and pants unseeingly. On the right, Phillip crawls across the floor, staining the expanse of whiteness with a vermilion trail. Phillip reaches for the knife, galvanizing Danielle to lunge for the weapon. In shadow, we see her stab him in the back again and again, her inhuman groans, screams, and sobs competing with Herrmann's pulsating chant-like Moog synthesizer and horns, shrieking strings, alongside clashing, tinny glockenspiels, "pull[ing] us into a vortex of chaos, death, and futility."[40] Finally, she hurls the bloody knife across the room and a slow pan brings us back to Phillip's limp, twitching body.

Why, at this climactic moment, does De Palma intellectualize his shot through reference to *Psycho*? In answer to this question, John Ashbrook quotes the man himself:

> Audiences are very much used to being told what they are going to see and feel, so they're very comfortable with that . . . But when you make a film that plays with form it throws a lot of people off. They're not used to playing with form the way we did in the 60s and 70s with Godard or Antonioni.[41]

De Palma's insistence on elevating visual grammar over emotional intensity at this key moment may seem cold, but as the above quote suggests, this is not to dampen the audience's enthusiasm but to estrange them from their expectations, to make them think as they feel, and thus think *about* what they feel and why.

This self-consciousness extends to *Sisters*' structural adherence to *Psycho*, as the seeming protagonist is murdered early in the film. "The underlying notion of setting somebody up and then killing them," De Palma argues, is to terrify an audience "by annihilating the very identification they have with the character they think is going to take them through the film."[42]

Minute 27

Not to be too grandiose, but Minute 27 will revolutionize film history. It's not the first split screen to appear in a film, but it's a moment of reinvention. The split screen device was previously used primarily in comedies to indicate phone conversations, in documentaries such as *Woodstock* to capture the collectivity and synchronicity of the event, in visual displays as in world's fair exhibitions, in films where one actor plays twins, and in De Palma's own experimental filming of the play *Dionysus in '69* to indicate the involvement of live spectators.

De Palma claims that before him, "no one has ever thought to use [split screen] as a dramatic form . . . ."[43] This is not entirely accurate—David Greven points to the early twentieth-century work of silent film director Abel Gance and Tony Williams mentions a 1968 predecessor in Richard Fleischer's *The Boston Strangler*—but it is true that De Palma's use of split screen at this moment marks a novum in cinematography, transcending the psychological and political depth of its past use.[44]

This technique continues to implicate the audience, while suggesting the complementarity and antagonism of the film's many pairings of doubles, "play[ing] with truth and time," observes Carrie Rickey.[45] De Palma refers to this choice as "a kind of Brechtian alienation . . . you're aware of what you are watching at the same time that you are emotionally involved in it."[46] Brecht himself defines these "alienation effects" as moments where "The audience can no longer have the illusion of being the unseen spectator at an event which is really taking place."[47]

In our first split-screen moment, a wipe transition halves the screen as Phillip claws his way to the window. On the left, we see the outside of Danielle's window, with Phillip's hand gripping the inside of the sill. On the right, Phillip is shown from behind, the back of his jacket smeared with bright red blood. The camera tilts up to see what Phillip can't. It's another apartment window, that of the woman he glimpsed last night. That woman is Grace who, following his death, will take up Phillip's role as *Sisters*' protagonist.

Sisters, as many have noted, imitates *Psycho*'s bold structure, intimately connecting the spectator to a protagonist who dies at the end of the film's first act. But few critics mention that our allegiances cross over to a new protagonist just as we see the film's first split-screen shot. That is, De Palma's formal innovation isn't just a stylized gesture, it marks the film's politicized break with convention. A Black man who has been treated as a joke, a servant, and perhaps a sexual object in the first third of the film does not just die. He hands off an agential torch to a leftist, feminist journalist who bears her own burden of oppression and prejudice. The split-screen technique keeps this solidaristic relation alive through the terrors, the comic mishaps, the tragic failures to come.

In this inaugural split, shots of dual windows both connect and separate Grace and Phillip. Only the audience can peer through both portals. The split-screen view augments this suggestive refraction, raising more questions than it answers. Who can see? Who can't? Does our gaze fetishize the victims? Are we doomed to passivity? Can our gaze intervene? Are these two characters enemies or twins? Allies or strangers?

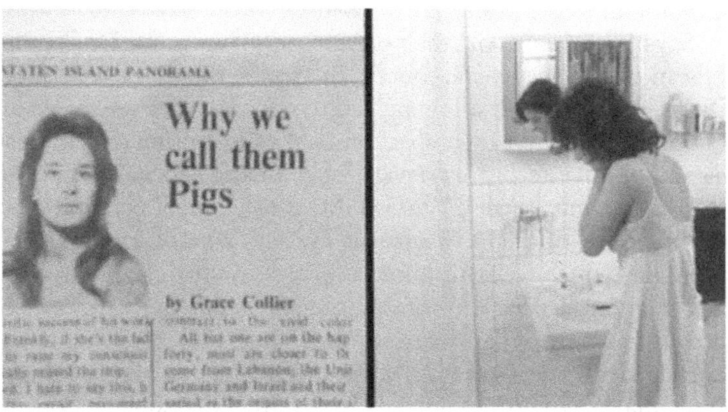

Sisters *directed by Brian de Palma © American International Pictures 1972. All rights reserved.*

Minute 28

Left half of the screen: Zoom out from Phillip scrawling the word "Help" on the window with his own blood (an image that haunted De Palma long before *Sisters* was conceived and was one of his inspirations for the film). The shot comes from behind Grace's shoulder, as she sits facing her window, "forg[ing] an empathetic link between the two characters," argues Douglas Keesey.[48]

Now from Grace's point of view, we zoom in on Phillip's bloody, flailing hand slipping away from the windowsill. With rapid-fire delivery, Grace phones the police and reports the emergency. As she speaks, the camera pans to her right, lingering on a series of framed newspaper articles written by Grace herself. The titles establish her as a politicized journalist for a local Staten Island newspaper. Our gaze lingers on an op-ed entitled, "Why we call them Pigs." We can't hear what the police say when she gives her name, but her calm response is telling—"Yes, *the* Grace Collier. I wrote that story . . . I'm sorry you feel that way Detective. But I have to write it the way I see it. Sometimes the police are wrong."

Says John Ashbrook, the point-of-view shot is, for De Palma, "far more than a stylistic conceit. By cutting the character out of the frame and simply allowing you to see what they see, you can temporarily inhabit their space instead of just using the camera as an objective recording device for dramatic action."[49] It's rare to give a woman this POV vision. At best she might be a sidekick to the holder of the POV gaze, as in *Rear Window*, where Lisa Fremont (Grace Kelly) is allowed access to "the gaze" through her relationship to Jeff (Jimmy Stewart). But here it's Grace herself gazing out her "rear window" and into her neighbor's homes. Her name, Grace Collier, grants her further Hitchcockian credentials—connoting Grace Kelly and Constance Collier, actresses appearing in *Rear Window* and *Rope*, respectively.

De Palma's tendency to complicate the gendered and racialized gaze in his films leads Linda Badley to boldly claim, "De Palma was thinking far ahead of Mulvey's white heterosexist male gaze,"[50] suggesting the famed feminist and reputed misogynist are, like Danielle and Dominique, complexly twinned.

As doubles, both Mulvey and De Palma wrestle with political disappointment following the 1960s. Gone is the revolutionary ferment that gave context to that decade's cinematic experiments. Argues Laurence F. Knapp, "Much of De Palma's cynicism comes from the political and social failures of the sixties: the assassinations, the conspiracies, and the ever-encroaching media, with its unyielding message of conformity and materialism."[51] Suffering this blowback, De Palma confessed his insurrectionary film *Greetings* came too late:

> **De Palma:** I found myself on talk shows, talking about the revolution, and I realized I had become just another piece of software that they could sell, like aspirin or deodorant. It didn't make any difference what I said. I was talking about the downfall of America. Who cares? In my experience what happened to the revolution is that it got turned into a product, and that is the process of everything in America. Everything is meshed into a product.[52]

Minute 28's split screen captures this contrast between collective hope and capitalist atomization. On the left, Grace, still tied to the remnants of counterculture leftism, is dynamic, active. On the right, Danielle, an institutional ward and wife, lies unconscious in her bathroom.

The juxtaposition is striking. Grace is efficient, matter-of-fact, tough, and driven by fairness, moving briskly to report what she speculates is a racially motivated crime. Her feminist, counterculture credentials are underscored by gritty chain smoking and a hippie-styled, unfeminine housedress.

On the other side of the split, Danielle lies supine, wearing a frilly, diaphanous nightgown, her voluptuous breasts nearly exposed. When she finally moves, it's with groggy torpor. Grace is an agential, modern woman, while Danielle is a feminine archetype out of a fairy tale, a dream, or a nightmare.

These polarities, though, form a connection. Asserts Robin Wood, Danielle and Grace are "two components of [a] composite 'monster' . . . in constant and unresolved antagonism." The split screen "simultaneously juxtaposes and separates the two women, presenting them as parallel yet antagonistic."[53]

Danielle gradually revives, unaware she has killed a man. Rubbing her head, she hoists herself up and looks in the mirror with confusion. A seam running through the middle of the glass divides her face eerily, "suggesting the division within her between repression and confession," Keesey proposes.[54]

Finally, lethargic and dazed, she makes her way to the door, called by a faint knocking. Emil's entrance onto the scene ends the split screen, erasing Grace from the spectator's view, severing Danielle's fragile connection to her agential, feminist double. With strange watery eyes, Emil looks over Danielle's shoulder, taking in the bloody scene.

Sisters *directed by Brian de Palma © American International Pictures 1972. All rights reserved.*

Minute 29

Minute 29 marks an irrevocable turn. Danielle and Emil realize their lives will change forever. Surveying the carnage she or her twin has wreaked, Danielle is paralyzed. Emil springs to action, pulling her away from the window lest she be seen. Grabbing a broom, he demands, "Help me." Previously, we saw Danielle celebrating her independence from her ex-husband. Now, it seems, she will be trapped with him forever, tied by complicity, blackmail, and guilt rather than love or desire.

Bill Finley, who appeared in most of De Palma's early films and who will go on to star as Winslow Leach in the director's next film, *Phantom of the Paradise*, plays Emil. In previous performances, he created comically psychotic, sexually ambiguous tricksters. Considering Emil's role as the patriarchal villain in *Sisters*, who dominates Danielle as her husband and doctor, we might expect him to radiate masculine menace. But he instead appears as a queerly oblique character, supporting David Greven's assertion of De Palma's deeply suspicious relation to masculinity.[55]

As an example, Greven points to the opening scene in De Palma's 1968 film *Greetings*, one of the few narrative films about the sixties made from within the counterculture. This film that Bartholomew notes "has come to stand for the '60s"[56] and Tarantino sees as a model of "late sixties zeitgeist authenticity,"[57] opens by showing real footage of Lyndon B. Johnson preaching to America's male youth about their necessary role in US aggression toward Vietnam: "I hope you men are determined to help us meet these problems and give justice to the people of this nation and the world . . . I'm not saying you never had it so good—but that is a fact, isn't it?"

Greetings goes on to depict a trio of countercultural friends seeking to dodge Johnson's draft. The film not only critiques the Vietnam War's cruelty, but widens its condemnation to encompass warrior-like masculinity in general. As Greven describes *Greetings*—"Its concerns hinge on the pressures to sustain and achieve national manhood, pressures which inspire racism and death wishes."[58] The film's protagonists resist the war effort, but they are more confused about their allegiance to masculine ideals.

Greetings' young, male protagonists rarely question their desire to dominate women and seem immune to empathy as they ignore, objectify, and abuse "the weaker sex." However, the film itself is concerned with and sympathetic to these women. In Greven's words, the young men's friendship reveals "the underpinnings of male bonding in America . . . a shared complicity in the brutalization of women and other men . . .."[59] Contra the common perception of De Palma as a misogynist, Greven asserts that this brutality "emerges as the crucial framework for [De Palma's] studies of all forms of gendered subjectivity."[60]

In *Greetings* Jon Rubin (Robert De Niro) is a voyeur who tricks women into stripping for him by claiming that they will star in an artistic film he's directing, a clear reference to De Palma's own role as a filmmaker/purveyor of the male gaze. Despite his friends' picaresque attempts to keep him out of the war, Jon ends up getting recruited.

The comic yet scathing ending of the film shows Jon as a lone soldier stalking the Vietnam brush, followed by a camera crew and a TV journalist narrating his actions. The announcer relays that Jon has spotted his enemy through the scope of his rifle. Jon informs the TV journalist and audience that he's going to kill the woman he has in his sights, since she's VC. Instead, though, he approaches her and instructs her to undress, using the same commands he had given to a previous victim of his voyeuristic, predatory scam. In an incredible montage, this footage of Rubin ordering the North Vietnamese woman to disrobe is crosscut with footage of a white woman whose trust he violated at home, stripping on her bed. Cut to the same clip of LBJ from the beginning of the film as he reprimands his young male audience: "I'm not saying you never had it so good, but that is a fact, isn't it?"

Returning to this opening quote at the end of *Greetings*, we come to understand its full meaning—participation in the

Vietnam War gives young men license to do whatever they want with women at home and abroad. Notes Angela Davis in an essay demonstrating the paradoxical relationship of "the myth of the Black rapist" to the entitlement of the white rapist:

> the experience of the Vietnam War furnished a further example of the extent to which racism could function as a provocation to rape. Because it was drummed into the heads of U.S. soldiers that they were fighting an inferior race, they could be taught that raping Vietnamese women was a necessary military duty. . . . It was unwritten policy of the US Military command to systematically encourage rape as it was an extremely effective weapon of mass terrorism.

Finally, Davis asks, as we do after watching *Greetings*, "To what extent did those brutal experiences affect their attitudes toward women in general?'"[61] Greven adds, "De Palma equates the Viet Cong woman's sexual exploitation with the militaristic exploitation of war and carnage, which the film has depicted as the culmination of masculinist cruelty."[62] Although few of De Palma's later films are so didactic, this sixties work looms large over the gendered and racial violence in *Sisters*, supporting Robin Wood's claim that the 1973 film is "a rigorous dissection of the egoism fostered in the male by the culture's obsession with 'masculinity.'"[63]

In an earlier De Palma film, *Murder a la Mod*, from which *Greetings* borrows key scenes, Finley plays Otto, the sexually ambiguous, comic foil to Christopher, the macho director/murderer character. In this experimental film, as in *Greetings*, the director's role is associated with a violent voyeurism literalized through murder. Finley/Otto is merely the decoy, or the comic relief. This could be a clue that in *Sisters* Emil is a humorously ineffective proxy for the more sinister effects of a male gaze structured by the director and enjoyed by the audience.

Some see De Palma's turn to the thriller genre in the seventies as a break from this overtly countercultural sixties cinema, but we can here agree with Dumas that *Sisters* works to popularize rather than reject leftist politics.[64] Finley serves as a bridge between the director's two phases, not only by "queering," or perhaps "enfreaking," his role in *Sisters*, but by refusing to assimilate to the thriller genre, instead performing as if he were in a Godardian farce.

Laurence F. Knapp sees De Palma's alienation effects, such as encouraging Finley's odd acting, as evidence of "'split cinema'—part identification, part distantiation . . . a product of De Palma's modernist sensibility and his efforts to synthesize commercial projects with his avant garde work in the 1960s." This "schizophrenic style" serves as a protest against "coercive" commercial media. If De Palma can't fully opt out of late capitalism's totalizing spectacle, he can at least "make you aware of how cinema can conceal and confound perception and the truth."[65] The director's job is thus to challenge the audience, rather than offering reassuring familiarities.

In his interpretation of Emil, Finley follows Brecht's dictum that the actor should "appear strange and even surprising to the audience . . . by looking strangely at himself and his work."[66] In addition to explaining his character's jolting gestures, this might illuminate why Emil is depicted as a spectator during so much of the film. We are introduced to him in the audience of *Peeping Toms*, and later he spies on Phillip and Danielle rather than intervening in what he should predict will be a murder. For the last half of the film, he looms like a sentient, expressionistic shadow, coiling watchfully over Danielle and Grace's supine bodies. Already, in Minute 29 he clings too closely to Danielle, as if he were an insectile parasite or yet another evil twin.

Minute 30

Emil's obtrusive role in *Sisters* also helps explain the tonally jarring slapstick scenes to follow. While Grace waits for the police, Emil and Danielle begin disposing of the evidence. But where to hide a body in a one-bedroom apartment? They lift Phillip and dump him on the bare wires of the sofa bed, folding him into the body of the couch and covering their crime with pillows.

This choice of body disposal cost De Palma dearly. The director implied that he lost studio funding because of this method when he said:

> Marty Ransohoff, who had run Filmways and considered producing the film, never believed I could put a corpse in a couch. He said it can't be done. I replied, "Yes, it can be done." He remained convinced that nobody would ever believe this was possible. So, I made it a big item in the movie. And it's really the actor we put in the couch; I did it in one shot.[67]

De Palma's intransigence regarding the couch/coffin may have been due to stubbornness or an impish sense of humor. However, Mark Olivier's *entire chapter* on *Sisters* and sofas in his book *Household Horrors*, convinces me that this is more than a prop, but "an accomplice to murder."[68] For one, Olivier suggests, the collapsing sofa connotes De Palma's preference for cinematic folding structures, not only evident in the misdirect that begins *Sisters*, but in other red period films like *Dressed to Kill* and *Blow Out* that challenge our perception by staging scenes whose meaning will soon be exposed or reversed. As Olivier cleverly puts it, the sofa "accounts for the ways in which the film unfolds and folds back in on itself, for the facility with which it toys with positions of repose and for the value of instability or duplicity as a defining design feature."[69]

This piece of furniture, an elision between the private, sexual bedroom and the public, social living room, becomes a dynamic and elusive pun. After Phillip is enfolded, he will never be seen again, but the sofa itself will be pursued throughout the film and will centrally occupy the film's final shot. In addition to serving as a reference to Hitchcock's *Rope*, in which the body is hidden in plain sight, the sofa is a clunky capitalist allegory, a commodity that subsumes a Black man. With this enfolding, social death is covered up, but the film never lets it go.

Minute 31

Minute 31 involves crosscuts between Grace, impatiently waiting for the cops to show up, and Emil erasing signs of Phillip's murder. Danielle goes to vomit in the bathroom, with Emil hot on her tail, insisting that she put on makeup. Emil is a campy figure, but he's not wrong that Danielle's contrived mask of femininity will be seen as a mark of innocence and normality.

Minute 32

Just as Grace opens the door to the cops, a wipe reopens the split screen. On the left, Emil assembles cleaning products to scrub away the copious blood spattered on the apartment's surfaces, including a thick trailing stain where Phillip crawled across the room.

On the right, Grace hurries Detective Kelly and Detective Spinetti into the lobby where she learns the cops are less interested in investigating her claims than belittling her

Kelly accuses Grace of imagining the murder, and Spinetti makes the racist remark—"Take it easy, will you lady. These people are always stabbing each other."

The split screen continues to posit Danielle and Grace as both doubled and contrasting figures. Danielle is filmed at a similar angle to Grace, but where Danielle is heavy lidded, Grace is alert; where Danielle is passive in her pink satiny robe, Grace is forceful in her rust-colored vinyl jacket. Still, Grace's agential stance doesn't stop the cops from infantilizing her. Quite the opposite. And, as we see from the split screen, every minute the cops waste brings Emil closer to successfully covering up a murder.

On the surface, the detectives' homosocial exclusivity is simple gaslighting, but we can read even more into this toxic behavior. Male friendship in the directors' films, David Greven asserts, "metonymically serves as the linchpin of De Palma's consistent, overarching critique of dominant forms of social control: governments, bureaucracies, special task forces, the military, the media, all depicted as spheres of homosocial power."[70] Elsewhere, Greven argues that in De Palma's work women operate as "the site of exchange between men" but also as a receding horizon against which men must prove their masculinity. The depiction of women, then, "is inextricably connected to [De Palma's] general critique of the compulsory performance of masculinity and manhood in American life."[71] Detective Kelly and Detective Spinelli bring this home as they focus on overpowering Grace rather than investigating a potential murder, proving once again the ever-relevant Public Enemy lyrics, "911 is a joke."

Minute 33

Minute 33 presents juxtapositions within juxtapositions as on the right of the split screen Emil's industrious cleaning is intercut with Danielle's laborious process of "putting on her face." Emil wipes a bloody floor with green fluid while Danielle brushes her lashes with mascara. Emil sponges a blood-spattered surface while Danielle carefully applies lipstick. Emil removes more bloody stains while Danielle dabs her cheeks with blush. Emil uses a cloudy spray to wipe the blood-scrawled words "help me" off a window as Danielle applies lipstick. Emil secretes bloody fabric in a garbage bag as Danielle lines her eyes.

If the dialectic on the left exposes two methods of "covering up," on the right we see the more overt political stakes of this moment as Grace struggles to save Phillip (who she believes may still be alive) while the racist cops resist her rational but increasingly urgent pleas. Says Linda Badley, this contrast "underscores characterization and theme; contrasting the narcissistic woman with the woman who uses the investigative gaze to seek justice; it literalizes the motif of dual identities."[72]

Detective Kelly's authoritarianism and sexism are on display as he changes the subject from the emergency at hand to Grace's journalistic exposé of police brutality. She's not a "real reporter," Detective Kelly insists. Translation: she should wait at home while the men take care of business. Perhaps in this moment Grace realizes that not only would these cops rather beat up students than save lives, as she outrightly accuses, but a more unspeakable reality—that, at core, the cops' "profession" is to maintain unequal power relations rather than to protect and serve. Screw the "experts," Grace resolves to investigate Danielle's apartment herself, heading out of the lobby and to the elevator. Only the desire to further chastise this wanton woman leads Detective Kelly to follow.

Minute 34

The split-screen persists. Danielle continues "putting on her face" as Emil comically attempts to clean. While taking out the garbage, he trips over his own feet and lands face-down on the floor. On the other side of the screen's border, Detective Kelly's imposing demeanor and physiognomy misdirect us to think he will easily prevail against Emil's slapstick clownishness.

As Grace and her antagonists approach Danielle's apartment, the split-screen shots meet spectacularly. In a dazzling innovation, both sides of the screen depict the same hallway from opposite directions. For a second, Emil crosses over from the left panel to the right and is almost caught by these keystone cops. But the detective has wasted too much time scolding Grace for her womanly, leftist "hysteria," ultimately allowing Emil and Danielle to get away with murder.

Sisters *directed by Brian de Palma* © *American International Pictures 1972. All rights reserved.*

Still, there is hope in this moment as Grace stands up to her detractors, refusing to be quiet, declaring, wishfully perhaps, "This isn't a police state yet."

Minute 35

And yet, we reach a threshold where Grace's feminist force is eclipsed by Danielle's feminine frills. The separate spheres of the split frames converge as the left side of the screen depicts Danielle facing Detective Kelly and Grace, who are shown frontally on the right side of the screen. The number and placement of the setups for this scene must have been awe-inspiring and excruciating.

In her satiny nightclothes and with her lilting French accent, Danielle begins her charm offensive—"If there is some information that you need, I will be glad to help you," glancing coyly down at her negligee. "But as you can see, I am in the middle of dressing." She goes on to soften her request for a search warrant by "forgetting" the proper term, calling it by the less demanding name "search permission."

Outshone by Danielle's conventional beauty and adorable passivity, Grace is entirely ignored. Dwarfed behind Kelly's shoulder, she attempts to assert herself, making the (correct) accusation—"She's stalling. She's hiding the body." Predictably, no one acknowledges Grace has spoken.

Notes Linda Badley, the split screen here works to "rupture the illusion," estranging the typical moves in classical Hollywood cinema.[73] Conventionally, the conversation between Danielle and Kelly would be naturalized by one of the most common techniques in mainstream film, the shot/reverse-shot—that is, alternating shots of the two people in dialogue from opposing directions. With this convention, when one person is shown, the other is either mostly or totally invisible. Shots are paced to follow conversational flow and facial reaction, and faces are generally shot in ¾ views. The use of eyeline match and of the 180-degree rule that orients the viewer by staging the conversation on a continuous axis are followed to imply that the gazes of the two participants are reciprocal, working "to suture viewers into the moment of the narrative through their identification with the point of view of the characters."[74]

A "naturalist" school of thought claims that shot/reverse-shot was adapted for its verisimilitude to the experience of human conversations. But David Bordwell claims this convention is "unfaithful to ordinary vision." In other words, this seemingly innocuous "invisible" continuity editing is more intrusive than it seems. Rather than observing objectively, this shot offers an idealized, omnipresent view, designed not "to call attention to itself, but to the story that it is telling."[75] Or, as Laura Mulvey puts it, creating "a hermetically sealed world which unwinds magically, indifferent to the presence of the audience, producing for them a sense of separation and playing on their voyeuristic phantasy."[76] Ultimately, suggests semiotician Kaja Silverman, the constructed gaze (using shot/reverse-shot) within a fiction serves to conceal the controlling gaze outside the fiction.[77]

Notes Silverman, the 180-degree rule of cinematic expression undergirding the use of shot/reverse-shot is "predicated on the assumption that a complete camera revolution would be 'unrealistic,' defining a space larger than the 'naked eye' would normally cover."[78] But this adherence to the "natural" rules of vision denies another reality, that this scene is mediated through the camera's gaze, instead "fostering the illusion that what is shown has an autonomous existence, independent of any technological interference, or any coercive gaze."[79] At the same time, the shot/reverse-shot directs us to imagine we are looking at the scene through the eyes of a particular character, rather than the camera. This is how the audience is sutured, or stitched, into the film's narrative illusion, concealing the apparatuses of enunciation, in this case, the camera. When the "code," as Daniel Dayan calls it, is thus disappeared, the spectator is at the mercy of its ideological effect, absorbing it unthinkingly.[80]

The camera's "coercive gaze" may seem to be an objective formal element of the film, but Silverman agrees with Laura Mulvey that the camera gaze and the male character's gaze are typically fused in classical Hollywood cinema, having the result "of attributing to him qualities which in fact belong to that same apparatus—qualities of potency and authority" while female characters who "are spoken, not speaking, and whose gazes are controlled, not controlling" signify the viewer's lack.[81] Psychoanalytically this equates to castration, the lack of the phallus. In other words, Silverman notes, it's impossible to consider "any part of the classic cinematic organization—including editing—apart from sexual difference," and this is most clearly shown in the shot/reverse-shot formation. Silverman characterizes deviance from this form of suture as a temptation to rebel—"to refuse cultural re-integration, to skid off-course, out of control, to prefer castration to false plenitude." In disrupting "classic cinema's scopic regime" this deviance points to "female resistance within the very system which defines woman as powerless and lacking."[82]

In avoiding using shot/reverse-shot when depicting the encounter between Danielle and Detective Kelly, De Palma subverts the smooth experience of continuity editing, and rather defiantly "skid[s] off course."[83] If the more conventional technique of shot/reverse-shot had been used during this conversation, shots from Detective Kelly's point of view would have emphasized the scopophilic pleasure he, as a figure of power and authority, draws from gazing at Danielle, a beautiful, scantily clad woman on the wrong side of the law.

A shot/reverse-shot would have confirmed Detective Kelly as the active investigator of both a murder and of Danielle's passive beauty. This typical filmic framing of male/female interaction upholds what Mulvey sees as the binaries ideologically defining sexual difference—passive vs. active, the one who looks vs. the one who exhibits, the phallically empowered vs. the castrated, narrative momentum vs. static spectacle. However, shot in split screen rather than shot/reverse-shot these binaries are troubled. Clear separations are dissolved, segmented only by a cartoonish seam between the right and left frame. This hyperbolic border broadcasts rather than conceals the constructedness of these divisions in the first place. As in Mulvey's call for deconstructive cinema, the audience member, now no longer an "invisible guest," will be liberated to engage in "dialectics, passionate detachment."[84]

Minute 36

Finally, Danielle allows Kelly, Spinetti, and Grace to enter the room. When the threshold is breached, the split screen disappears in an abrupt cut. A side is chosen, and it is the side of closure. After our wild split-screen journey down Alexander Hamilton's warmly lit hallways, we are returned to and contained within Danielle's antiseptically white apartment as well as cinema's traditional rules emphasizing continuity and unity. The characters obediently arrange themselves along a 180-degree axis and tilt their heads just so to achieve an eyeline match with their interlocutors. Danielle, hitherto depicted as a warm and complex woman, is flattened into a standardized femme fatale whose innocent demeanor and sex appeal conceal a killer. And now that the murder scene has been sanitized, it sinks in that our would-be protagonist—the generous, genteel, sexy, ambitious Phillip—is dead forever, unceremoniously stuffed in a sofa on which Danielle casually perches. Here, the end of the split screen might as well be the end of possibility—for anti-racism, for feminism, for the counterculture, for love, for any kind of livable world.

Minute 37

In Minute 37 Grace is finally permitted to make her accusation. In Grace's mind, her case is airtight—Grace saw a murder. She's certain it took place in Danielle's apartment. Logically, then, a murder in Danielle's apartment irrefutably happened, and Danielle is now covering it up. Given the unimpeachable, concrete evidence Grace's eyewitness provides, the situation is cut and dried. There is just one problem. Grace doesn't suspect that Danielle is the killer. Not at all. This beautiful, glossy woman who sits before Grace couldn't possibly wield a deadly knife.

> **Grace:** The murderer is someone this girl knows. She was shorter and had a twisted face and stringy hair and was having a terrible fit of some kind.

Grace's confusion speaks to an unfathomable divide between the two women. Though Grace and Danielle live in the same neighborhood, are roughly the same age, and even look vaguely alike, they operate in irreconcilable spheres. Grace inhabits a daylit world where injustice can be fought through political battle. The feminist gains of the sixties and early seventies have given her the potential for autonomy. She, at least during the first half of *Sisters*, is pragmatic, akin to the Midge character in *Vertigo*, a rational witness to a psychotic narrative. Because of this, unlike most other female character types in Hitchcockian thrillers, Grace is permitted the right to *look*. As a journalist she is, in fact, trained in observation. She has earned this access to the gaze and she has faith in it.

Danielle's reality, on the other hand, evades the only kind of investigating Grace knows how to do. Her suffering can't be addressed by a law, a journalistic detail, or a political campaign. The psychic programming she has endured is now too entangled with her identity to be exorcised. Danielle's "truth" is not visible to the naked eye. Despite her singular body, she has been split into two women—virgin and whore, passive and active, sheep and slaughterer, "normate" and "freak," singleton and conjoined twin.

Grace won't stop until she "sees" this murderer and brings her to justice. What she doesn't realize is that to truly see Danielle she must enter the schizophrenic realm of dream logic and nightmare transmission where Dominique dwells. As she will learn, to see Dominique is to be Dominique. That is, to be insane.

Minute 38

We can read Minutes 37 and 38 as a meditation on the dialectics of "watching." While it is true that Grace's 20/20 vision doesn't allow her to "see" what lurks beneath the surface of Danielle's smooth exterior, it is also correct that Grace *did* witness Phillip's murder and that Danielle intentionally and persistently lies about that fact.

Detective Kelly: Could somebody have gotten in here without your knowledge?
Danielle: It would be impossible. I was here all morning.
Grace: What about the man that stayed over?
Danielle: I was quite alone. You see I'm . . . I'm divorced from my husband, and still uh . . . Well it's very personal

> you know. But Miss Collier, many times at night I watch the television show . . . and I watch the horror film, and it make me full of fear, and I jump at every noise. I understand that when you live alone it make you—It's very difficult. I understand that.

In this dialogue, Danielle basically calls Grace an isolated spinster whose "truth" is a delusion. However, in gaslighting her accuser by explicitly mentioning a horror film, Danielle paradoxically points to the *untruth* we are all experiencing at this very moment, watching *Sisters*. The film's narrative is not "real." We are watching a horror movie. But in the context of Danielle's false accusation—in which she uses the idea of a horror movie to lie and conceal the truth of Grace's experience—this discrediting of horror films is itself a lie. So, is the hidden key to reality found in a lonely woman's experience of watching horror movies late at night? Asking for a friend . . .

Minute 39

Danielle finally gives Detective Kerry permission to search her apartment. Grace rushes to investigate, and Kelly leaps to prevent her. Leading her to the sofa, he sardonically tells her that he knows she's trying to help "the forces of justice" but the best service she can do is to passively sit like a good girl. Grace won't be deterred, insisting the corpse is in the apartment and Danielle knows where it is. The camera deliberately leads our eyes to a bloody smudge left on the couch by the hapless Emil. But even this prominent evidence of Phillip's murder won't be found by our clueless detectives.

Grace follows the cops to inspect the bathroom and then feigns a need to use the facilities, a ruse to sneak back to the living room to search for the body without Danielle and the police present. The camera shoots Grace from behind the shower curtain for no apparent reason. This shower perspective, I'm guessing, is De Palma's wink at critics who will call him a mere Hitchcock knock-off.

Yes, this movie (another thriller scored by Bernard Herrmann in which the protagonist is murdered at the end of the first act) has seen *Psycho*, it loves *Psycho*, it will happily provide an homage to *Psycho*. However, *Sisters* is also using the tools provided by *Psycho* to tell its own story. The flowery blue and green shower curtain is the bathroom's only instance of color. In fact, it is one of the few signs of life in Danielle's austere white apartment. Yes, it is a shower curtain, but it looks completely *different* from *Psycho*'s white, plastic, translucent shower curtain. This shower curtain, De Palma seems to say, has a sense of imagination and humor even if the judgmental critic does not.

Minute 40

Did I mention Danielle is transient, a woman with no true home? Grace sneaks into her living room to rifle through one of the many unpacked boxes lining the living room walls. Other than the cursed sofa bed, a glass coffee table, and a white lamp placed haphazardly, the room is empty save for brown packing boxes. Her brief new life, away from the institution for "freaks," away from Emil, will be over before it began.

When Grace is forced to join the detectives in Danielle's bedroom we see that the room designated for rest, intimacy, and desire, too, is unlived in, unhomey, *unheimlich*. Nothing here but a bland bed, a closed trunk, and an open suitcase. Hotel-anonymous white dressers blur into clinically white walls. Say what you will about Danielle's conventional femininity, she does *not* keep house. No man will have his dishes washed nor his babies reared by Danielle. Harboring nearly nothing but a bed, a couch, and a corpse, Danielle's anonymous dwelling is a place for lounging, sleeping, fucking, murdering, and little else.

Minute 41

Grace insists on checking the hallway closet and Danielle agrees. No accompanying soundtrack tells us how to feel. Save the "shower scene," the apartment search has mostly occurred on neutral sonic ground. As Danielle ceremoniously opens the hallway closet, we remain in silence. However, when Grace unzips the translucent clothing bags hanging in the closet, Herrmann's sinister score creeps in. The bags in the closet, suggesting queer secrets within secrets along with, yes, *Vertigo*, contain identical pairs of white dresses, which we guess are Danielle's and her twin, Dominique's.

Throughout this police visit, despite her skimpy negligee, Danielle has appeared fully clothed in her armor of makeup and charming broken English and flirtatious mannerisms, but when Grace unzips these bags, Danielle, too, comes undone.

Grace opens a bag and looks at the off-screen detectives in triumph. This—the pairs of identical dresses she discovers—shows that Danielle's claim to live alone is a lie. Even more telling is what Grace can't see. Close behind Grace, Danielle, smothered in Grace's shadow, lets her mask of confidence fall.

When Grace accuses Danielle of having a twin, the latter is quick with an excuse. In her work, she says, she needs "back up" clothes in case she sullies the outfits she uses for work. But Grace is onto her.

In another brilliant staging of reflexivity, one actress (Kidder), who is playing a murderer claiming to be an actress (Danielle), says to another actress (Salt): "You see, I'm a model, and sometimes an actress too." Grace retorts: "You certainly are."

Minute 42

Detective Kelly reprimands Grace for her rudeness toward Danielle, driving home that decorum matters more to these cops than a Black man's murder.

And that's that. Detective Kelly apologizes for having "troubled" Danielle and is about to be on his way. The bulging couch, pregnant with a dead man and sporting a large bloody stain on its pale surface, will remain unnoticed, even as it sits in the center of the small apartment's most prominent room. Instead of observing his surroundings, Detective Kelly milks the last few seconds of this visit by offering the lovely Miss Breton stern, fatherly advice to refrain from withholding evidence, lest it make her "an accessory after the fact."

The detectives' exit, however, is momentarily hindered by the arrival of Emil. Danielle politely introduces the men, while Grace absconds to the kitchen, a room the cops haven't bothered to inspect. We view her through the back of a cutaway icebox painstakingly designed to give this brief shot an uncanny view of what Marc Olivier calls the "cold womb" of the kitchen, a distinctly feminine space where "heat must be perpetually thrust aside in order for the refrigerator to live."[85]

In the sparsely stocked fridge, Grace spots Danielle and Dominique's birthday cake. This is a breakthrough—the appearance of both sisters' names on the cake confirms the existence of Danielle's twin. In her eagerness to display her evidence, though, Grace stumbles, dropping the frilly cake on Detective Kelly's foot and rendering her "proof" illegible. This, the film's second pratfall after Emil's slip-up while cleaning, is a comic intrusion into a tensely structured atmosphere. Like the *Psycho* shower curtain, physical comedy works as a form of estrangement, denying the viewer immersion in cinema's magic illusions; instead, forcing us, as Brecht would require, to think as much as we feel, and to think about why and how we feel.

Minute 43

Grace is on her knees trying to reconstruct Danielle and Dominique's cake by mashing it back onto its cardboard base. By now, we know the dogged Grace will never give up her pursuit of justice, no matter how futile her efforts seem. But here, for the first time, she looks defeated. Not only is she in a servile position, crouching at Detective Kelly's feet, but her voice falters as she explains of the evidence, "it was right . . . right here."

Cut to the exterior of the Alexander Hamilton apartment building where Detective Kelly, fully in possession of the upper hand, dispenses with pretense, reveling in the cop's entitlements—aggression, corruption, authority. If Grace says one more word, Kelly threatens, he will find a pretense to arrest her. He ends his tirade by scolding, "Listen, Miss Collier, I don't know what kind of a nut you are or what kind of an exposé you're looking to get. But just don't bother me or that girl upstairs, okay? Far as I'm concerned, the case is closed."

Here, Detective Kelly manages to trivialize Grace's left-wing journalism and invoke her "female hysteria" at once. At the same time, he harkens back to racist "chivalry" by "protecting" lily white Danielle and ignoring the alleged death of a Black man. Despite the promises of the sixties' social movements to leave the draconian fifties' authoritarianism behind, the seventies' United States is still no country for young women, unless they trade in their hard-won independence, feminism, and anti-racism for a passive smile and a silky nightgown.

Minute 44

Grace immediately enters another circle of hell as her mother appears, pouncing like a shrill, tastefully coiffed tiger stalking her prey. We learn that the mother and daughter had a scheduled date, and that witnessing a murder is no excuse for missing it. Naturally, instead of waiting outside, Mrs. Collier barged into Grace's empty apartment, "and if you were embarrassed about the mess, you know I'm always glad to help you tidy up. . . . Although what you're going to do when you get married, I don't know."

Yes, she's *that* kind of mother (played, incidentally, by Jennifer Salt's actual mother, Mary Davenport). And, not incidentally to the film's anti-capitalist themes, Jennifer Salt's father is Waldo Salt, the left-wing, blacklisted screenwriter who made his post-McCarthy era comeback scripting brilliantly critical films such as *Midnight Cowboy*, *Serpico*, *The Day of the Locust*, and *Coming Home*.

The tense body language and immediate bickering between the two women exhibit a lack of trust, but even more telling is that Grace doesn't recount the horrific ordeal she has just been through. Instead, she tries to humor the judgmental older woman. Continuing her passive-aggressive onslaught without noticing Grace's distraction and dismay, Mrs. Collier suggests that Grace isn't dressed appropriately. Grace immediately agrees to change outfits, unveiling the unequal mother/daughter power dynamic casting a shadow over her adult life.

Dissolve to a long shot of a car, driving on Staten Island streets. Through the window, we see Grace listlessly smoking, her blank face turned away from Mrs. Collier.

Cut to car interior. Grace remains facing away from her mother who is obliquely reminding her of her inadequacies—"Oh did I tell you the Cunningham girl is engaged? She's about your age and she finally found somebody that suits her. He's a doctor. Well, he's a veterinarian, but the animals are all owned by wealthy people."

Clearly, Mrs. Collier is prepping Grace for a Cinderella-like transformation into a conventional woman, married to a rich man, raising his children. As she obviously has many times before, Grace tunes out.

In this disjunctive moment between conventional housewife mother and independent journalist daughter, *Sisters* shows itself to be an unambiguously second wave feminist film in which our heroine is not only pursuing justice for a murdered man but fighting to escape the fate of a Stepford Wife.

We will never know the extent to which *Sisters*—the most consistently feminist of De Palma's films—was influenced by its co-writer Louisa Rose, the director's friend from his days at Sarah Lawrence, but her contribution seems much more significant than has been noted. In a rare interview, she describes the process of building up the script:

> He had kind of an outline. He had this idea that it would be twins, one evil and one good sister. . . . You know, it's just so long ago it's hard for me to remember. There were certain points, certain visual things he wanted. We worked together on the story, and then *I wrote the script* (emphasis mine).[86]

Even more telling is a detail from a long interview with De Palma, taking place at the American Film Institute. At one point, the director is asked what Rose's contribution is to the film.

> **De Palma's response:** I wrote the script initially for Ransohoff, and then Louisa went back and rewrote most of the women's scenes because she built all the women's characters. And that was a great weakness for me because I don't write women too well. And she wrote them very well.[87]

This is a bombshell *since literally every scene in Sisters foregrounds the women characters*. These revelations deeply challenge auteur-focused discussions of *Sisters*, showing the film, from its inception, to be a true collaboration with women, even if these women were under-credited for their creative contributions.

Despite this accomplishment and her work on De Palma's subsequent film, *Phantom of the Paradise*, Rose didn't go on to have a Hollywood career. She traveled as a single mother to LA to work on the film and was put off by De Palma's delays in (under) paying her as well as by her encounters with Hollywood's near ubiquitous sexual harassment.[88] Nevertheless, Rose's participation in *Sisters* as well as Jennifer Salt's and her mother's improvisations during this key scene convinces me that the film's feminism was in part a product of women's creativity and collaboration not only as actors but also as writers and shapers of the film's direction.

Minute 45

Mrs. Collier's commitment to human sacrifice (in the form of marrying off her unwilling daughter) is not where her insidiousness ends. More than that, she's a well-rounded guardian of the bourgeois conservatism so pointedly and consistently challenged in De Palma's sixties films.

This painfully conventional woman pivots from nagging Grace about her spinsterhood at the ripe old age of twenty-five to complaining about an "experimental madhouse" that somehow evaded zoning laws in her neighborhood. The idea of an asylum allowing "crazy" people to "walk around . . . like real people" in her back yard is so offensive she's even willing to admit her daughter is a reporter, although she remains as condescending as possible—"Are you listening honey? Because this would make a very interesting story for your newspaper."

Mrs. Collier's dehumanizing stances in favor of patriarchal conventionality, bourgeois respectability, moral panic, redlining, carcerality, and intolerance of the mentally ill make her a perfect intersection of everything *Sisters* is against. We have plenty of evidence of De Palma's anti-authoritarian bent in his early films *The Wedding Party*, *Greetings*, and *Hi, Mom!*—critiques of bourgeois marriage, the Vietnam War, and racism, respectively. While some of his approaches to these topics are dated, De Palma, at this point in his career, was all in for the left. Adrian Martin and Cristina Álvarez Lopez explain, "De Palma is a product of the 1960s—of its counter-cultural currents, and its political upheavals." Martin and Lopez go on to describe De Palma's early films as

> low-budget, anarchic, scattershot, semi-improvised films that "act out", in comical-grotesque terms, the various obsessions, anxieties and liberations of [the sixties] as De

> Palma experienced and internalised them. Some version of Women's Liberation jostles with paranoiac fears over vast government conspiracies and cover-ups; the sudden intermixing of racially white and black cultures on home turf intersects with the war in Vietnam.

De Palma's fantasy at the time sums up his political and aesthetic commitments—"If I could be the American Godard, that would be great."[89]

Some critics argue De Palma's swerve from Godardian didacticism to Hitchcockian thriller led to apolitical formalism or selling out. But *Sisters*' narrative unconventionality, its experimental framing and cuts, its defiance of continuity and unity, its comic intrusions, are aimed, if not at shocking the bourgeoisie, then at seriously pissing them off, taking aim at soul-deadening middle-class complacency responsible for everything from the Vietnam War to police brutality to women's subservience.

Before we leave Minute 45, let's return to Mrs. Collier's complaint about the "mad house" invading her neighborhood from another angle. The appearance of this institution as the film's "terrible place," as Carol Clover would have it, points to the historically entrenched corruption of *Sisters*' setting, Staten Island. While writing this book, I came across a 2009 documentary, *Cropsey*, created by two lifelong residents of the borough. Cropsey is a typical urban legend, a deranged psychopath who steals and murders children. But it turns out he is a stand-in for Staten Island's horrific legacy as a dumping ground, not only of millions of tons of waste in its landfill, but of people—dead people, sick people, mentally ill people, old people, unwanted children, those seen as human trash.

In 1972, the year of *Sisters*' production, another Staten Island-based film was made. This was an investigative report called *Willowbrook: The Last Great Disgrace*, helmed by Geraldo Rivera, then an idealistic left-wing journalist, exposing a Staten Island facility for developmentally disabled people as a horrific cesspool of abuse. The institution, opened in 1948, presented itself as a place of care, but Rivera found the patients, many of them children, abandoned, covered in their own shit, riddled with hepatitis and other ailments, without even their basic needs met. Says Rivera: "how can I tell you about the way it smelled? It smelled of filth, it smelled of disease, it smelled of death." Yet, the institution's most enduring legacy wasn't a moral lesson learned from its maltreatment of its wards, but the urban myth of one of its "caretakers," Andre Rand, thought to be Cropsey. The murderer was said to be driven mad and desensitized by the monstrosities he was party to at that institution. The legend of Cropsey, then, exemplifies horror's function of monumentalizing repressed social terrors.

And Willowbrook was just one example of Staten Island's reputation as a wasteland. The mob dumped corpses in its rivers and graveyards; a tuberculosis ward held dying people behind its walls; the state of New York sent all its trash, twenty barges a day, to Fresh Kills, the biggest landfill in the world—1,284 acres—up until its closure in 2001, after having taken in 2,000 tons of trash per day for decades.[90] Even after it closed, Fresh Kills macabre legacy accrued as the former dump became a sorting ground following the Twin Towers attacks, where experts looked through 1.6 million tons of rubble, ultimately retrieving the remains of 4,257 people, only 300 of whom could be identified. As of 2023, "it is highly likely that this debris still contains fragmentary human remains."[91] Extending both into the past and future of *Sisters*, then, Staten Island contextualizes the film's themes linking personal and institutional violence.

There's no evidence De Palma intentionally selected Staten Island as *Sisters*' shooting location because of this history. In an interview, Jennifer Salt speculates that the location was chosen because it felt more intimate and was cheaper than shooting in Manhattan.[92] However, De Palma did create a muckraking local reporter for *Sisters*' protagonist who investigates a version of Staten Island where vulnerable people are immured in abusive institutions. That is, consciously or not, *Sisters* is another urban legend built on a haunted mass grave.

Minute 46

True to her reporter instincts, Grace noticed the bakery where Phillip bought Danielle's incriminating birthday cake. She spots the shop from the car and orders Mrs. Collier to pull over. Released from her mother's infantilizing hold, Grace is back in the driver's seat. Still, the older woman persists in her relentlessly classist patter, following Grace onto the sidewalk and complaining about the bakery's soggy pastries.

Ignoring this distraction, Grace marches into the shop and approaches a saleswoman. After Grace jogs the woman's memory, she vaguely remembers that morning's customer. She thinks the names she wrote on the cake were Daisy and Debbie, but her co-worker corrects her, "Dominique and Danielle." When Grace mentions she's a writer for the *Staten Island Panorama*, they gaze at her with respect—"My Girlfriend and I read your column!"

Let's pause to revel in this rare non-claustrophobic moment of *Sisters*. Grace is out in public space, exhibiting her confidence and competence. She is aided in her quest by two working-class women, who respect her accomplishments and seem to feel solidarity, as they themselves are independent women (one played by Olivia Dukakis, known in the sixties as a Brechtian stage actor). In contrast to the constant gaslighting we've seen Grace endure, for a minute she is validated as she gathers information confirming Phillip's murder.

Enjoy it while you can, because, of course, this respite can't and won't last. Hopes for solidarity recede as we detect racism and xenophobia in the salesladies' attitudes toward Phillip and the foreign-coded names on the cake. With these unsavory clues, even the bakery's sweetness sours. We rightly suspect this brightly lit moment primarily serves to contrast the darkness to come.

Minute 47

Grace gets the information she needs from the saleswomen and goes outside to write down her notes, hounded by her tirelessly annoying mother, whose critical commentary never ceases: "Really, Grace, you were rather abrupt."

Following her demoralizing encounter with the detectives, Grace was pliant with her mother, but now that she has been proven correct about the cake, she has the energy to defend herself: "I happen to be working on an assignment."

Mrs. Collier goes for the jugular: "Well don't you think you're taking this little job of yours a bit seriously? You're twenty-five years old. You should be thinking about something else."

Grace rises to the occasion: "I'm not gonna marry anybody. And I wish you'd stop referring to my work as 'a little job.'"

Before we move on, please enjoy this moment of political clarity granted the character who in the script was dubbed "the Gloria Steinem of Staten Island."[93] Made three years before *The Stepford Wives*, *Sisters* advances a similar message to that feminist horror classic. Modern women want independence and careers. They want the choice to opt out of a wifely role. When Mrs. Collier refers to Grace's "little job" she reminds us that normality, as Robin Wood argues, "is still marriage, the family and patriarchy—all that the monster of the horror movie has always implicitly threatened."[94] For Wood, *Sisters* is a great film because it dares to make its "monster [Grace] emerge as the most sympathetic character and its emotional center." That is, "one can define the monster of *Sisters* as women's liberation . . .."[95]

Some contemporary feminist critics considered De Palma's films misogynistic, but Linda Badley insists these films

> were *about* misogyny. . . . De Palma was the only New Hollywood figure to consistently foreground the gender politics inherent in the language of cinema—while targeting

> contemporaneous feminist hot-button issues with the instincts of a provocateur.[96]

In this view, the director's ironized presentation of masculinity and femininity raises issues of "the gaze, identity, and gender in terms of their potential for performative play with the cinematic apparatus, genres, and roles."[97]

Badley's and Wood's analyses rebut Quentin Tarantino's interpretation of *Sisters*' relation to feminism. Instead of taking Grace's serious attitude as representing her hard-earned feminist dignity, which will be tragically undone as the film progresses, Tarantino sees Jennifer Salt as the movie's weak link because, sigh, she didn't get the joke. That is, she didn't understand that her character was supposed to *be* a joke (and perhaps needed this mansplained to her). Tarantino instead thinks De Palma's intent was "to present his women's-lib reporter protagonist as a pigheaded, self-righteous ass."[98] "If you pay attention," Tarantino snarks, "you might even notice that a couple of [Salt's] lines are written to be funny. But Salt's delivery just bulldozes over any comedic intent."[99]

But Quentin, if what you are saying is true, then the whole film is really a joke—Grace's mission has no stakes, we need not care about her sacrifices to investigate the murder of an unmourned Black man, her critical interventions into a seemingly impenetrable web of patriarchal institutions are meaningless. The only reason to watch the film is to admire De Palma's dedication to "pure cinema" and passively receive his "calling card" as a great auteur. I'll just say here that I disagree with Tarantino's reading of Salt's performance—which I see as understated and wry rather than humorless and clueless—and leave it at that . . ..

Okay, one more thing. Tarantino is not alone in his dismissal of Grace as a humorless feminist. The 2018 Criterion Blu-Ray release of *Sisters* features a lengthy 1973 audio discussion between De Palma and a (mostly male) audience at the American Film Institute. Some of this recording is inaudible and we don't know who participated, but at the outset, one man irately interrogates De Palma about what he sees as a gaping hole in the film's quality, that the Grace Collier character/ Jennifer Salt actress comes off as "a little dumb," reminding him of "a thing I've known from girl reporters in New York. . .." De Palma's response is endearingly loaded with mystified exasperation—"You think Jennifer Salt is dumb?" His tone makes it obvious he thinks the actress is undeniably brilliant and that his interlocutor is a rube.

Throughout the interview, this critic asserts that Grace is clueless, incompetent, boring, and unsympathetic. He claims she is not introduced with any characterization, even though we witness revealing glimpses of her journalistic interests and her relationship with her mother. Throughout the hour-long recorded discussion, this man persistently reiterates his revulsion toward Grace, incorrectly suggesting that the blundering minor character Larch, included for comic relief, should have been given more prominence since his competence can be contrasted to Grace's ineptness. And later he (or another man in the audience) accuses De Palma of creating unrealistic police characters since they are more interested in scolding Grace than investigating a murder, missing *Sisters*' anti-authoritarian message altogether.

Today, fans understand *Sisters* as an example of what Jordan Peele calls the "social thriller," featuring societal, rather than supernatural demons. In a popular review on Letterboxd, Mia Lee Vicino welcomes *Sisters* as an "addition to ACAB canon." Black Lives Matter and the daily news have taught us that cops will not save us from crime, and rather stand in the way of justice.[100] This was no less true in 1973, but here, De Palma's audience can't see it.

At one kind of heartbreaking point in the aforementioned recording, this pestering critic proclaims that he can't identify with any of *Sisters*' characters because they are all "sick or stupid," a statement that seems to include the perfectly "chivalrous" Phillip just because he is Black, as well as the justice-seeking Grace just because she's a leftist feminist.

When, in response to the critique that the film is too bloody, De Palma later suggests that the murder scene *should* be traumatic, the critic is clueless—"why should it be traumatic?" De Palma responds—"The audience identification is dying. It should be upsetting. Maybe not for you, but certainly for me." You can hear in De Palma's voice a slight edge of disgust that his interrogator can't conceive of identifying with a murdered Black man.

Finally, when it becomes clear that the audience has missed all of the film's feminist and anti-racist themes, and can only praise its formal achievements, De Palma wears down, and half-heartedly agrees that the story could have been more comprehensible with more time and a bigger budget.

This discussion with supposedly sophisticated film critics and filmmakers shows the barriers a 1973 film like *Sisters* faced. And yet, many feminists of the time would not leap to *Sisters* defense against these clueless men, even if the film was on their radar (as De Palma's later films would become, to his chagrin). The crude masculinism of the AFI critics and Tarantino is the flipside to the blunt feminism of the second wave feminist anti-sex, anti-porn movement that protested De Palma's later films. Both reductively miss the director's reflexivity. This was a moment "where radical feminists and the 'moral majority' became uncomfortable bedfellows."[101] If seventies chauvinistic male critics wanted a movie with white male protagonists with whom to identify, seventies feminist critics demanded only sanitized heroines. These women attacked De Palma for depicting women experiencing sexual violence or practicing sex work, assuming that these depictions were always aimed at pleasing a sadistic male gaze.

Yet, even in the seventies, and more so now, sex-positive feminists assessed De Palma's representations of women more favorably. Argues Thomas Leitch, De Palma shows "surprising sympathy for the problems of women"[102] Linda Badley adds that De Palma's women are just doing their job, surviving in a "sexual economy in which they will be subjugated as long as late capitalism continues."[103] De Palma's women are often victims or hustlers, but this is simply a realistic result of the limited social roles on offer. Women are made, not born.

Minute 48

This is one of those minutes that puts the commie-tinged red in De Palma's "red period" (the period spanning 1973 to 1984 beginning with *Sisters*, in which the director focused on erotic thrillers). Beyond rejecting women's limited roles as wives and mothers, Grace attacks the barriers she faces as a journalist. We learn she got into the profession to fight for social justice, but found herself barred from taking on the causes she cares about. She's angry at her mom for insulting her "little job," but she must admit the assignments she gets from *The Staten Island Panorama* fall short. She complains: "I'm having lunch tomorrow with an eighty-year-old ex-con whose just carved an entire replica of the Danbury penitentiary out of soap." In other words, she's forced to write a trivializing puff piece about New York's sadistic prison industrial complex when she wants to investigate, she exclaims, "the apathy in the police force . . . where the heroin goes after a bust . . . the fat political cats!"

Grace feels impotent rage at this rampant capitalist collusion and corruption, but her small-minded mother is more concerned with propriety. Shushing her daughter, she says worriedly, "You don't have to shout right here on the street. What's the matter with you? I've never seen you like this." Grace is so excited about her investigation that she almost answers honestly, but her mother cuts short her enthusiasm with the patronizing question, "Are you on diet pills again?"

Chastened and repulsed, Grace tries to exit the scene while smoothing things over, postponing the mother–daughter date. Finally, Mrs. Collier lets herself be dismissed. As she walks away muttering, we see she is less hurt by her daughter's rejection than she is mystified by the disorder of it all, "Well it's not the way I planned it, but if that's the way we're gonna do it . . .."

The stark contrast between Grace and her conformist mother marks *Sisters*' continuity with De Palma's sixties films which, he said, "are about the obscenity of the white middle class."[104] In the seventies, De Palma's style transforms, but this radical commitment remains. He maintains, as Dumas puts it, "a Godardian orientation toward the Hitchcockian object,"[105] a political continuity missed by leftist critics who equate De Palma's retro genre citations with older, reactionary ideas, and assume that "movies that resemble older movies are implicitly of [an] older ideological order."[106]

This may be true in the case of the most famous New Hollywood directors, like Steven Spielberg, but De Palma's red period films and (sometimes) his later work remain darkly critical. Says Dumas:

> the deep mistrust of family relations that typifies De Palma's output from *Sisters* to the *Black Dalia* is surely indicative less of a conservative shift toward the family than of a recognition—theorized out of Marcuse, or Godard, or Hitchcock, or merely personal experience—that the roots of both social and personal oppression are born in the family and, therefore, always return there.[107]

In minute 48, the toxic family structure, exemplified by the tension between a housewife mother and a feminist daughter, becomes a metonym for "the system," including De Palma's own fears of Hollywood's market-driven production enterprise.

De Palma's first disastrous encounter with that system was his involvement with Warner Bros' studio film *Get to Know Your Rabbit* immediately before he made *Sisters*. The huge amount of capital required to make a studio movie meant artistic autonomy had to take a backseat during this production. Warner Bros. ended up forcing De Palma to make unwanted changes and took three years to release the movie. Says Tarantino: "After the bad studio experience of *Rabbit*, De Palma realized, by 1970, the sixties hippie aesthetic was dead on arrival. But De Palma's entire identity was tied to that aesthetic."[108]

This disappointment, says Dumas, was De Palma's "'primal scene', the traumatic moment that breaks his career into a before and an after . . .."[109] In Hollywood, De Palma laments, "you have to use tremendous sums of money to do what you want to do, you're dealing with a huge capitalistic structure. And capitalism exploits. You become corrupted."[110] *Sisters* and *Phantom of the Paradise*, then, form "twin allegories for De Palma's own experience in Hollywood . . .."[111] The former shows a reporter who is banned from telling any real stories, and the latter depicts a musician exploited, deformed, and murdered by a corrupt entertainment industry.

Securing support for *Sisters* was complex and rife with disappointments. De Palma's first foray was with Filmways, a studio known for TV production, but also for interfering with directors' creative choices. The head of the company, Martin Ransohoff, helped to distribute De Palma's early counterculture films, which encouraged the director, despite some red flags, notes Tarantino.[112] But then Ransohoff sold De Palma's scripts to another producer, Raymond Stark, known for bullying and "mangling more films than an El Paso drive-in movie projector," as Tarantino put it.[113] When Stark suggested casting Raquel Welch for the film's lead, De Palma bowed out. In the end, *Sisters* was produced by Ed Pressman, just some guy who used an inheritance from his parents' toy factory to become a producer. Finally, the film was sold to AIP, but De Palma had to make compromises due to budgetary constraints and the imperative to make a commercial film, or else become a Hollywood exile.

These compromises came at a moment when De Palma couldn't go back to what he was doing before Hollywood. The New Left movement and counterculture that inspired and supported the director's earlier independent films was disintegrating. *Sisters*, as what Dumas calls "the cinema of failed revolt," reacts to these disappointments with themes steeped in futility. Phillip's unmourned death and the unceremonious disposal of his corpse capture a moment when the police have no interest in investigating the death of a Black man, nor is there any collectivity to protect or honor him.

Still, *Sisters* exhibits traces of countercultural desire by refusing full closure into the genre conventions De Palma explores. Rather than following the typical structure of a thriller, asking and answering the rote question: who committed the murder?, the film wants us to consider genre as a contract that must be signed, but is destined to be broken. We identify with Phillip, only to see his death ignored and covered up. All the "unbound social forces which gave the 60s their energy," as Fredric Jameson names them, are now folded back into the sofa bed and put to sleep.[114] Ghostlike, we inhabit the aftermath of political awakening as a "traumatic break" after which films as well as film theory are created in "the shadow of disappointment."[115]

Still, Grace refuses to go back into the closet of convention and submissiveness. Her mother wants to continue driving her around (and driving rather than riding as a passenger is a sign of dominance in this movie), but Grace declines. Wherever she's going, she's getting there on her own.

Minute 49

Having wrested herself from her mother's nagging hold, Grace goes to a phone booth to call her editor. Now that the bakery employees have corroborated her story, she feels empowered to investigate what she sees as a politicized murder—"A white woman kills her Black lover and those racist cops couldn't care less!," she protests to her interlocutor.

We don't hear the response, but we know it's dubious because Grace threatens to publish with another paper before she is given grudging permission to pursue the story. However, the editor doesn't seem to trust her to proceed without a man's help. She is forced to hire a private detective, despite her pleas for autonomy—"I know more than those idiot police." Not incidentally to the scene's ongoing feminist themes, we learned from a previous conversation with her mother that Grace's editor is also her disappointing lover or ex-lover.

The next shot will introduce us to the private detective, Joseph Larch. Like the cops, he frames Grace as a rookie, whose amateurism he contrasts with his own professional knowledge. Also like the cops, this condescension will be belied by Larch's bumbling incompetence.

I want to describe the camera movement in this moment as churning. A creeping 180-degree pan arcs around Grace as she argues with her boss/lover in a glass phone booth that could be a cage. This is followed in the next scene by another, somberly paced and lengthy pan from Danielle's apartment window to a truck where Grace and Larch bicker. If *Sisters* introduced the gender divide as a dramatic split screen, these lethargic pans point to an ongoing banality of low-key sexism, entrapment, and gaslighting. As it goes in a society guided by uninterrogated patriarchal rules and mores, wave after sluggish wave of the camera's panning gaze subjects Grace to perpetual, near-undetectable vertigo and surveillance. Like a frog boiling by minute degrees in water, Grace will never know the precise moment where her liberation was sacrificed to these gradually encircling forces.

Minute 50

If you are still skeptical that *Sisters* is *about* sexism rather than sexist, look to the film's comic bits for confirmation that not only is the film on Grace's side, but that she is in on the joke (and it's De Palma's male critics who often miss it). Grace and Larch's dynamic is a rapid-fire exchange in which the detective simultaneously interrupts and shoots down every suggestion made by the reporter. They are now debating how to infiltrate

Danielle's apartment, and to be honest, neither one offers a convincing plan. Both are drowning in pop-culture detective narratives, and both contrive hairbrained schemes such as making a wax impression of a key or communicating by elaborate hand signals. However, the difference is that Grace is willing to consider her shortcomings while Larch is certain of his mastery. When "logic" fails to convince Grace of his scheme's superiority, Larch flaunts his credentials, boasting of his training at the Brooklyn Institute of Modern Investigation, which doesn't sound even a little made up. Unsurprisingly, Grace's response lacks adequate deference. As she exits the truck, he mutters, exasperatedly, "girls," infantilizing and generalizing her at once.

Minute 51

Larch's plan triumphs, of course. Grace is to return home and check out Danielle's apartment from her opposing window. If the apartment is empty, she will signal to Larch and he will break in, disguised as a window cleaner. This part goes as planned. He enters the empty apartment, and she follows his progress through binoculars, as he moves from room to room, finding nothing.

We might read this *Rear Window* tribute as a "good for her" moment, since it's filmed through Grace's active gaze. We see Larch and the apartment through her binocular lenses; that is, through her prosthetic eyes. Yet, the moment is more comical than affirmatively political. We can't help giggle at our overturned expectations when we see an attractive woman spying on a dumpy man in janitorial coveralls (played for laughs by the working-class character actor Charles Durning). Maybe this farcical inversion of Hitchcockian voyeurism hints to us that the penetrative gaze is not something to be democratized, but deflated. With laughter if possible.

Minute 52

In the seventies, Laura Mulvey's theory of the male gaze as presented in her essay "Visual Pleasure and Narrative Cinema" dominated feminist film theory. Now, few cite Mulvey's precepts without reacting critically to them. Maybe her diagnosis of illusionistic narrative film's patriarchal bias has become so commonplace that many feminists don't feel the need to foreground its points. More concerning to many is what Mulvey's theory *doesn't* account for, such as the status of a female or queer gaze. This isn't the space to retread such debates, but for the purposes of analyzing *Sisters*' feminist themes, I want to reaffirm Mulvey's basic premise, that the cinematic gaze is structured to accommodate male pleasure and to placate the male fear of castration (even if it's possible for individual women and queer people to appropriate or resignify these gestures). I eagerly anticipate the day social structures are revolutionized, and patriarchal logic no longer undergirds narrative and cultural forms, but that day has not yet arrived.

All this is to say, it's naïve to imagine Grace's act of surveillance can singularly defeat the inequality structuring how and for whom one looks. Yes, it's true that here we see Grace actively surveying Larch and at Danielle's apartment, but the moment's satirical tone belies any fantasy that representing a woman peering at a man translates into a powerful "female gaze."

This doesn't mean, however, *Sisters* promotes political hopelessness or quietism. As Grace stares through her binoculars, we glimpse a blurry poster behind her. It's a portrait of the militant Marxist, anti-racist, feminist Angela Davis. The activist stands proudly and seems to be in the middle of a political speech. If Grace can't succeed as a "strong female lead," her relationship to the collective resistance Davis signifies is more promising. Even if Grace succumbs to the patriarchal forces encircling her (spoiler alert, she will), she won't go down without a struggle. The poster reaffirms our intrepid reporter's ongoing allegiance to the countercultural leftist forces that opposed racism, war, and patriarchy through the sixties and will continue to do so even in the face of failures, disappointments, and recuperations. Grace herself may fall, but her fighting spirit will persist, proclaims Walter Benjamin, in the "confidence, courage, humor, cunning, and fortitude" of class struggles to come.[116]

Minute 53

Point-of-view shots; women seen through glass windows; women speaking on telephones with no one on the other end. All of these *Sisters*' staples occur in Minute 53. Such tropes are integral to De Palma's meta-cinematic handbook. Characters are cropped by windowsills as if they are on a screen, which they also are. Acts of looking, hearing, and speaking are filtered through devices such as binoculars and telephones, drawing attention to their mediations as well as to the characters' failure to communicate. These are not empty formal gestures, but prompts for the spectator to reflect—Who is looking? Why are they looking? Why are you looking at them? How are they framed and why? How are you complicit in this framing?

Minute 54

Danielle and Emil catch Larch in the apartment, but fortunately they buy his cover as a window cleaner, and he escapes unscathed. We don't see this directly, but glimpse fragments of the story through Grace's lenses, piecing the rest together on our own. Larch next appears helping two workers load the sofa—pregnant with Phillip's body—into a moving truck. As soon as Danielle and Emil retreat, Larch gleefully runs to his van where Grace waits.

Larch hands Grace a file he found in the apartment and begins following the moving truck. As Grace rifles through the file's contents, Larch confirms her suspicions. There was a body, and it was hidden in the couch. He knows because the couch was very heavy. The way he relays this information exhibits Larch's masculine insecurity. Since he couldn't lift the sofa, it *must* contain a body. At every turn Larch belittles Grace, adding gratuitously that he believed she was a delusional hysteric until *his* investigation confirmed the corpse's presence. As in many of the scenes where Grace faces overt patriarchal behavior (with Larch and her mother), this scene was improvised, showing the creative and political contributions of the whole ensemble, and forcing us to question auteurist readings of the film.

Why Larch doesn't expose the dead body now, solving the mystery once and for all, I'm not sure. In response to this question, Larch would likely remind me that my small woman-brain lacks the acuity to follow his complex and highly trained logic.

Minute 55

Assaulted by Larch's blustering self-aggrandizement, Grace can barely get a word in edgewise. But still, she makes her own discoveries. In the file, she discovers evidence that Danielle was one of the infamous Blanchion twins. She tries to explain the significance of her findings, but Larch cuts her off with more braggadocio. Imagining himself involved in a grandiose scheme, he assumes the corpse will link to a conspiracy. His plan is to follow the couch/coffin to Quebec where he's certain there will be a colluder waiting to receive the body, and where the larger plot will unfold.

On the one hand, Larch's conspiratorial projections reflect his masculine need to be part of something bigger than the interests of a "lady reporter." But he isn't entirely wrong. What Grace has discovered *is* more than just a local incident. Phillip's death is not just the death of one man, it's a symbolic end of an era. The Victory Van line containing the body, emblazoned with the words "World Wide Moving," suggests Phillip's corpse is now destined to merge with capitalist global circulation, a system extending beyond Larch's or Grace's perception.

That is, the conspiratorial imagination is reactionary, but it also contains a grain of truth. Our neocolonial era of market forces creates "a growing contradiction between lived experience and structure," says Fredric Jameson.[117] In the face of this overwhelming scale, Frank Ruda notes the irony that "conspiracy theories are the wrong form of doing the right and necessary thing," which is to understand an incomprehensible world.[118]

Still, lost in his paranoid logic, Larch is useless to the problem at hand. Grace now has a lead on the Blanchion twins, but Larch isn't listening. Since he cuts off every sentence she utters, he has no idea of her plan to follow up on her own. Larch's preference is that Grace passively wait at home for him to carry out the investigation, and so that's what he assumes she will do.

In other words, Grace will soon need help, but no one will be around to hear her scream.

Minute 56

If Larch's conspiratorial thinking is useless for the kind of cognitive mapping needed in this situation, Grace's sense of the big picture is more on track. The Blanchion sisters, we will learn, were conjoined twins who separated as young women. Their case attracted the morbid curiosity of the nation.

Having traveled by ferry to *Life*'s Manhattan offices, Grace approaches Arthur McLennen, the reporter who originally wrote about the Blanchion twins. He recognizes the sisters' original medical files, and is thus willing to talk to Grace, even though she is only a small-time local journalist. Like the Victory

Van Lines moving truck transgressing national borders, Grace has crossed a threshold. The murder of Phillip by Danielle no longer seems to be the singular act of a madwoman, but a social phenomenon bleeding into unbounded horizons.

Minute 57

For Robin Wood the horror film monster represents everything that is repressed or oppressed. The genre, Wood suggests, allows the unspeakable to speak. Jeffrey Jerome Cohen adds that the monster in horror "is difference made flesh, come to dwell among us." Cultural, political, racial, economic, sexual difference, pushed down into the depths, erupts in the monster.[119]

Minute 57 is the first moment of *Sisters* where we learn that Danielle is not just a killer, but a monster. We had a hint in Minute 15, when we saw the huge ugly scar on her thigh. But here we learn the origin of this scar. This beautiful young model was once an outcast, a freak, a conjoined twin. When McLennen wrote a national news story about her and her twin, Dominique, the magazine received hundreds of letters, all with the "same tone of morbid fascination." McLennen admits that he too treated the sisters as dehumanized objects of curiosity, until he got to know them and became interested in their thoughts and feelings as well as the sociology of how they were treated. McLennen's transformation could be a lesson for the spectator on how we can retrain our gaze, from violating and penetrative to sympathetic and curious. But will we?

Minute 58

In Minute 58 McLennen shows Grace a documentary about the Blanchion twins, *Blanchion Twins Separated*. The viewer is not simply told it exists, we see the entire grainy, 16mm, black and white film within the film (assembled by future film critic and screenwriter Jay Cocks).[120]

The documentary begins with the words "Blanchion Twins Separated" in stark white against a black backdrop. Through a series of dissolves, still images of various conjoined twins are shown as both fragile infants who "challenge life at their first breath" and medieval etchings of "the stuff of myth and symbol." Even as the film explores conjoined twins who have tried to live ordinary lives through attaining families and employment, the images of their success are accompanied by Herrmann's eerily dramatic score, emphasizing their "strangeness." The viewer is shown conjoined twins who have been separated and gone on to "lead normal lives" as well as dramatic looking "freaks" whose bodies are so entangled that they will never be "cured" nor integrated into society. This is the context through which we are introduced to the Blanchion sisters, shown on an operating table as infants, "Canada's first Siamese twins" born in 1948.

This film within the film further estranges the act of looking, denaturalizing the primary film's formal choices by presenting other ways of seeing. Says Abigail Lynn Coykendall of *Sisters* and other De Palma films of this era, De Palma's definitive use of the "'point of view' shot" as "a technique that simultaneously evokes, captures, and suspends what generations of feminists have infamously deemed the 'male gaze'"[121] is further estranged by the "'interior' diegesis" or "'film within the film.'" The short films inserted into De Palma's features, she argues, typically "antagonistically rival[] the meanings unfolding in the larger 'primary' film."[122]

In other examples provided by Coykendall, De Palma's films within films are pornographic. But in *Sisters*' version of this trope, an equation is made between the pornographic male gaze and the medical male gaze, with beautiful young women who are also conjoined twins or "freaks" offered up as scientific experiments. The documentary form presents them as unmediated "evidence" of difference and monstrosity. But the documentary itself will be exposed as a sleight of hand, contributing to De Palma's deconstruction of the gaze's seeming "truth."

Sisters *directed by Brian de Palma* © *American International Pictures 1972. All rights reserved.*

Minute 59

Minute 58 gave us background on conjoined twins as a phenomenon, in the style of an educational documentary. Now Minute 59 focuses on Danielle and Dominique's particular story. We are shown a photo of mom cradling the girls as infants, then immediately learn their parents died in a car crash shortly after they were born. Following this tragedy, they were brought up "within the pale walls of the Loisel institute." We witness a photo of a masked nurse feeding two babies from a bottle, and a picture of them as children, sitting on a couch. Here the difference in the sisters' personalities is beginning to emerge. One girl, who we will come to know as Danielle, appears cheerful, social, and alert. Her twin Dominique bears a sullen, listless expression.

Incidentally, the image of the girls as children is staged, but it's based on a photo of conjoined sisters, Masha and Dasha, from Russia. One sister looked "as sunny and cheerful as can be, while the other had a darker and more disturbing expression."[123] De Palma credits this picture that he saw in a 1966 *Life* article as the spark igniting *Sisters*.

Now, the twins appear as grown women wearing bathing suits, still sweet and sour. The narrator informs us the two were inseparable due to their delicately conjoined spines. As this is described, the camera pans over the photo, and Grace recognizes Emil in the background, wearing a white doctor's coat. It begins to sink in (to Grace and to us) that Emil is not only Danielle's ex-husband but her doctor as well.

The director of the institute, Dr. Pierre Milius (an oppressive authority figure probably named after the right-wing film director John Milius) offers his opinion of the twins' psychology. He fears that as they age, their psychological balance is becoming more precarious, "both within themselves and between one another." While Milius's colleagues see Dominique as a disturbed contrast to the stable Danielle, the director disagrees. He thinks Danielle's "normality" that is so starkly juxtaposed with her sister's antisocial demeanor, is actually a sign of lack and interdependence. Remarking on his credulous colleagues he says, "I think they will find that Danielle, who is so sweet, so responsive, so normal, as opposed to her sister, can only be so because of her sister."

This pop psychology rings a bit hollow, but the implications of this symbiosis will resonate throughout the film. *Sisters* is replete with multiple pairs of female doubles—Danielle and her conjoined sister when Dominique was alive, Danielle and her phantasmal sister now that Dominique is dead, and later Grace and Danielle, as well as Grace and Dominique. In this way, *Sisters* is a palimpsestual exploration of the double's gendered uncanniness—in Freud's words: "relating to what is familiar and comfortable, [yet] concealed and kept hidden."[124]

The doubling between sexually available Danielle and sexually repressed Dominique also links to the old patriarchal classic, the virgin/whore dichotomy. This split evolves into a violent struggle within Danielle, exhibiting the cost of women's deadly repression, isolation, and self-alienation in the service of male fantasy. Despite their intimate proximity, all of *Sisters*' doubles are antagonists, suggesting women's alienation from solidarity in a world designed for men's pleasure and comfort. In a context where lone women are inserted "between men," women who "connect"—physically, psychically, or emotionally—with other women are ostracized as freaks. As we will see, the only way conjoined sisters (i.e., united sisters) can escape the "pale walls" of institutionalization is to sever their bonds in favor of heterosexual marriage, or die.

Minute 60

In the film within the film, Milius approaches the sisters as they sit by a therapeutic pool. The voiceover tells us this footage marks the twins' final public sighting. Rushing through the end of its tale, the documentary recounts that the evening after this interview, "nature" forced the doctors to perform an operation separating the sisters, even though they had previously ruled the procedure life threatening. The next day, the institute tersely and gloomily announced their success: "Dominique and Danielle: once one, would now stand each alone." And yet, we see no evidence of these autonomous women.

Following the film's abrupt ending, McClennen tells Grace about his attempts to follow up his research on the twins. Both the Loisel institute and his own employer prohibited his investigation, signs that powerful forces wished to control or bury the story. Here and elsewhere, *Sisters* is keen to distinguish individual journalists from their complicit employers. Like Grace, McClennen secretly persisted and finally contacted a nurse involved with the sisters' operation. He learned that Dominique died that night on the operating table, meaning that the Loisel institute is involved in a shocking cover-up.

With this revelation, *Sisters* compels us to question the nature of truth and its relation to cinema. The documentary style of the film within the film implied authenticity but ended with a blatant lie. The Falsehood was endorsed by *Life*, one of the most esteemed magazines published in the world's most powerful nation. Such institutionalized mendacity hints that even though Larch's conspiracy theory was off base, Phillip's mysterious murder *is* interwoven with complex and obscured power relations.

But not only did the documentary deceive, so did Grace's eyes. She had been certain she witnessed a different woman than Danielle committing a murder. Now it dawns on her that the killer and the sweet, feminine woman she met in Danielle's apartment must be one and the same.

Minute 61

If you were to watch this moment detached from the rest of the film, you would think you were in a movie about urban loneliness. And you wouldn't be wrong. First, a wide slow pan of a ferry against a darkened, anonymous Manhattan skyline; dissolve to a close-up of Grace's hand anticipatorily tapping a telephone; pan to Grace's remote expression as she smokes in shadows, watching and waiting; pan back to Grace's tapping hand; cut to a wide shot of Larch sitting in his tenebrous van staking out a forsaken diner that could have been painted by Edward Hopper; pan to the silhouetted pay phone from which Grace will never receive Larch's call.

Minute 62

Sisters isn't only obsessed with visual mediation; verbal communication is also estranged. Hence, the film's obsession with telephones. In Grace's apartment, we not only see her peering through binoculars but reaching out time and time again through her telephone (always to no avail). In Minute 62, Larch makes visual contact with a payphone but fails to make the call that could have rescued Grace from future terrors. In a few minutes, we will find ourselves in a clinic for the insane, where a madwoman spouts paranoid theories involving germs leaking through telephone receivers. The film will end in a bleakly comical scenario of Larch perched on a telephone pole, spying on the abandoned murder couch, at the dead end of his quest to unravel an imaginary conspiracy. *Sisters*' thread of what Marc Olivier calls "telephonic horror" suggests that though phones are considered an instrument of communion, the anonymity and physical distance characterizing phone communication lead to missed connections rather than reciprocity.

In film noir, Olivier notes, phones are employed "as a metaphor for isolation, violence, and alienation." He refers here to the "phone fatale," offering both attractions and threat.[125] In films such as *Sorry, Wrong Number*, phones point to an unseen "tangled network" binding isolated people together with the hope for interaction but also with a dread of vulnerability.[126] In *Sisters*, phones are never used for intimate relationality but for failed transfer of information, for intrigue, or for trickery as in a scene where Grace phones Danielle to distract her from Larch's unauthorized presence in her home.

Both the telephone and binoculars we see in this moment are prostheses, but with different connotations. Unlike masculine-coded scopophilia, sound and listening are often feminine-coded. This dichotomy of sight and sound maps onto semiotician Kaja Silverman's reading of cinematic sound as signifying feminized abjection, to be contrasted with the masculine rationality of visuality. For Silverman, sound is contiguous with the psychoanalytic function of the maternal voice, a "sonorous envelope [that] grows out of a powerful cultural fantasy . . .."[127] Sound attaches itself to the abject morass of the maternal, excluded from paternal rules and meaning.[128] There is thus mystery and fear accompanying sound. In particular, the telephone is, thanks to its ring, "a jump scare waiting to happen."[129]

In Minute 62, though, the phone remains unrung, the tension is unresolved, and the viewer is left with an ominous image of Larch driving into the night.

Minute 63

Grace again wields the binoculars to observe Danielle and Emil leaving their apartment, then quickly jumps into her car to pursue the murderers through empty streets, accompanied by Herrmann's suspenseful ostinatos. Emil and Danielle drive a station wagon, a vehicle more likely to be associated with suburban families than with foreign criminals on route to an insane asylum. This is another moment in *Sisters* where assumptions surrounding "normalcy" are upended. Grace is sympathetic, but not the "normal" one in this cat-and-mouse game. Instead of conventional, she is curious. Grace knows very well her prey are potentially violent, but remains steadfast and unruffled as a chill evening wind blows through her hair.

Minute 64

Driving, in *Sisters*, is connected to women's control. Previously, trapped in her mother's car, Grace was helpless against Mrs. Collier's nagging assault; Danielle always travels in the passenger seat of cars, and not coincidentally, is given no autonomy from the men in her life. In Minute 63, Grace drives her own car, maneuvering calmly and effectively through city streets. Minute 64 hints this agency won't last.

When Grace exits her vehicle, her independence is also left behind. The camera acknowledges this shift by filming the monstrous asylum from behind Grace's shoulder, rather than from her point of view, depriving her of the gaze while emphasizing the incommensurability of scale between her small frame and the huge, looming building.

From a distance, she witnesses Emil and Danielle arguing in French. Danielle tries to resist as her ex-husband/doctor shoves her into the ominous building, to no avail. Not only does this demonstrate Danielle's precarity, but Grace's as well. Until she spots Emil and Danielle, Grace walked purposefully toward the asylum. Now she cowers behind a bush. She can watch but can do nothing to prevent the unspooling institutional and intimate violence that besets Danielle.

Minute 65

This asylum is a version of Carol Clover's "terrible place," an ominous, looming, familial, swallower of unwitting victims whose "dawning understanding" of its atrocious history cements their own doom.[130] Its menacingly bland walls condense the nightmares of second wave feminists like Grace. All who are socialized into traditional womanhood know that the imperative to be a good wife and mother is followed by a silent "or else." "Or else" you may be institutionalized, stripped of autonomy, drugged, confined, chained, straitjacketed, disappeared.

Still pursuing Emil and Danielle, Grace runs to the building and peeks in a window where a scene from this gothic nightmare unfolds. Offscreen, we hear Danielle's untranslated cries to let her go—"Lasse-moi, lasse-moi." A medium shot of Emil throwing Danielle onto a couch, bearing down on her. Danielle emits loud, harrowing moans as Emil thrusts a needle into her chest. Cut to Grace, pressed up against the outer wall beside the window, disturbed, trying not to be seen. A close-up of Danielle's drugged face and limp body, Emil still looming over her. He lowers his head as if about to force a kiss, but instead stands up, wipes his glasses, and pulls out the plastic-wrapped bloody knife Danielle used to kill Phillip, as Grace looks on. Perhaps Emil keeps this knife as leverage over Danielle. Perhaps the knife is more than evidence, rather a mythic signifier of gendered violence.

The punctum of this moment is a bulletin board hung in the room—wildly dissonant with the moment's tone—where someone has affixed pictures made to soothe a restless patient—a gentle woman's portrait, a lovely sunset.

Minute 66

Emil unwraps the knife and Grace shies away from the window. We hear a snap and see the silhouette of a blade encroaching on Grace. Luckily, this is not a murderer's weapon but a pair of gardening shears held, with no ill intent, by a patient. When Grace asks what he is doing, he responds: "I have my work to do."

Later, we learn the "act of nature" leading to Danielle and Dominique's separation was Danielle's pregnancy, which Dominique aborted by attacking her sister's womb with a pair of garden shears. In retrospect, then, we're witnessing Grace enter phantasmal space structured by Danielle's unconscious. This transition is facilitated, notes Olivier, by Emil pushing Danielle into a supine position on the couch, a metonym for psychoanalysis.[131] Here, all objects double as Freudian "dream work," elliptical clues relating to Danielle's primal trauma of separation.

But these clues will only make sense later. At this point, we connect the gardener's free-ranging behavior to the experimental clinic we heard about earlier from Mrs. Collier as she relayed her NIMBY complaints about a madhouse invading her suburban neighborhood. From context, we can see this man is an inmate of the asylum, but he is also freely walking around outside and is even granted access to sharp gardening tools. Everything about the conversation between the man and Grace is banal and "normal," except his weird affect, her whispering, and the fact that, surrounded by bushes, he ceaselessly cuts at nothing but air.

Whereas earlier we could deduce from Mrs. Collier's conservative disapproval that this institution signified a progressive experiment, we are now asked to look at the situation from a different perspective. We are, I think, meant to see the "normal" activities practiced by its patients not as freedom but as a signal that everyday life is not so different than a madhouse. In a conformist capitalist society, banal, seemingly autonomous activities are underlain by coercion. There is not, after all, much difference between the madman's manic, compulsive gardening and conventional waged labor. Grace asks the man, "do you live here?" He answers, "so they tell me." This evokes Robin Wood's evaluation of the "crazy" hillbillies in *Texas Chainsaw Massacre* of whom he says, "The monstrous cruelties of the slaughterhouse family have their more pallid reflection within 'normality'"[132]

Minute 67

The paranoia running through *Sisters* captures this dark side of everyday life. As Grace enters the asylum she encounters Arlene (played brilliantly by stage actor Catherine Gaffigan) whose compulsions evoke a stereotypical housewife. Like a Stepford wife, this woman is obsessed with cleaning, but her attention is particularly focused on sterilizing the telephone Grace sees as a lifeline. A nightmare version of the domestic angel Mrs. Collier is trying to coerce Grace into becoming, Arlene appears, wild-eyed, in a flowered housedress, wielding an aerosol bottle of Lysol.

As she blocks Grace from the phone, Arlene's facial expressions run the gamut of emotions—manic cheerfulness, threatening ire, conspiratorial wiliness, sorrow, and terror—all within this one moment. A clear example of *Sisters*' "telephonic horror" comes when Arlene asserts that telephones are vectors of horrifying germs—"I never call and I never answer. It's a good way to get sick." Isolation and sterilization are the only escapes from contagion. Grace, she increasingly sees, is a contaminating threat. As if sounding an alarm, Arlene loudly announces the cause of her affliction: "That's how I got so sick. Someone called me on the telephone!"

Arlene's rising hysteria attracts an attendant to the room. When he demands to know who Grace is, she calmly states her name and credentials. But we can see from her placement vis-à-vis the attendant, parallel to Arlene, that Grace has already lost her authority and that she will be conflated with this madwoman.

Minute 68

Grace insists on speaking to the head of the clinic, threatening to expose the institution for letting a murderer walk loose. Although he admits "there have been a lot of wild rumors going around" about the asylum, the orderly seems genuinely confused by Grace's accusation. Finally, he picks up the telephone receiver, to Arlene's shocked dismay, and calls the director, letting him know that "a girl who says she's a reporter from *The Panorama*" is insisting on seeing him. While they wait, the attendant placates the still-sobbing Arlene, "You did a good job cleaning up. Now you can take your things back to the supply room." The warm kitchen, the paternalistic man, the hysterical housewife, all appear as "normal" life, told slant. Arlene edges out of the kitchen, making prolonged eye contact with Grace. Her back is to the camera so we will never know what this mad woman's gaze communicates to Grace, her double and antagonist.

Minute 69

Excepting her red hair, Grace couldn't be more distinct from Arlene. Where Arlene is emotional, paranoid, hysterical, Grace is crisp, direct, professional. But none of this matters when the clinic's director is revealed to be Emil. Grace insists that Emil is a murderer, and that the orderly must call the police. But Emil is ready for her. He calmly introduces her as Margaret, a new patient who was checked in the night before—"we're very happy to have her join our family." Instantly, the orderly's expression turns paternalistic. He now treats Grace with the condescending gentleness he had reserved for Arlene. Emil introduces the heretofore unnamed orderly as "Mr. Jansen," giving him, a man of about Grace's age, further authority over "Margaret" through the formal title.

Grace still thinks she has the upper hand—"If you'll go and check my I.D., it's in my car outside. I am Grace Collier." But as soon as she says it, she knows Mr. Jansen will never check her car, will never take her word over Emil's, no matter how rational and substantiable her argument. Emil takes Mr. Jansen aside, conspiratorially advising him not to insist on calling her Margaret right away. The two men turn to face her with a common, smug front. "We want to respect your wishes," says Emil, "When you are ready to have us call you Margaret, you tell us."

The men won't even give Grace the respect of arguing with her. She's slowly registering the shift; she's no longer a human with rights and choices, but a patient. Nothing she says will be believed. Any protest she attempts will only serve as further proof of her delusions. Here, eighty years and two waves of feminism later, the patriarchal strategy of diagnosing disobedient women with "hysteria," famously narrated in Charlotte Perkins Gilman's "The Yellow Wallpaper," endures.

In Gilman's day, the "cure" to hysteria was confinement and rest, whether in a domestic setting or an institution. The theory was that intense learning and strenuous exercise would destroy "that subtle and tender feminine charm which was the only source of masculine love . . ."[133] Of course, this lack of stimulation drove women crazy, ensuring a built-in confirmation of the diagnosis. Any deviance into the intellectual path of "the shrieking sisterhood" would lead women to become "sterile flowers doomed to bring forth only blossoms of hysteria and neurasthenia."[134] In other words, Emil and Dr. Jansen finish the job begun by Detectives Kelly and Spinelli, diagnosing Grace's feminism as a malady, to be cured at all costs.

Minute 70

"Come with me, Margaret," coaxes Mr. Jansen. As if there weren't enough instances of women's doubling in this film, now the authorities are calling Grace Margaret. She can't convince them she's a journalist. She can't convince them she's sane. She can't even convince them she's Grace. As if to emphasize how doubling diminishes women, during much of this conflict neither Mr. Jansen nor Grace are shown directly, but rather as black silhouettes against a bleak white wall, enacting a shadow play as old as gender.

Grace has hard evidence that she is who she claims to be—"Just go downstairs and check my bag. It's in my car." But of course, she is met with more patronizing skepticism. Mr. Jansen doesn't believe *her*, but he does, he assures "Margaret" with smarmy finesse, "believe you're serious in what you think."

In a move that is somehow worse than refusing to call this former professional journalist by her name, the men *do* call her by her name, but only to humor her. Grace is put into a position where anything she says becomes its opposite.

Grace: "Stop calling me Grace!"
Mr. Jansen: "Then you really do want to be Margaret?"
Grace: "No, damn it, my name is Grace."

When he does say it, Mr. Jansen injects so much treacle into the name "Grace" that it ceases to be hers. Instead, masculine authority dubs her Margaret—a formal, old-fashioned name, perhaps the name of the perfect little housewife Grace's mother has been pressuring her to become.

Now Mr. Jansen drags "Margaret" from the institution's Potemkin kitchen to a clinical room lurking behind this façade. There, with no traces of solidarity, waits a female doctor, wielding a long, aggressive needle. Mr. Jansen closes the door on the camera and on Grace's screams, isolating her completely, enclosing the viewer in blackness.

Minute 71

Against the darkness, we see what first looks like a murky light penetrating the black screen. But as the illuminated circle grows larger and closer, it reveals itself as an iris-wipe-in opening onto an extreme close-up of Grace's closed eyelids. From offscreen, Emil instructs Grace to open her eyes, and as soon as she does, a counter-shot pivots to Emil's face, seen through a distorted, fisheye lens emphasizing Grace's disorientation. Earlier we learned of Emil's plan to hypnotize Grace, and now that she is under his spell, he sets about indoctrinating her with the lie that "there was no body. It was all a ridiculous mistake. There was no body because there was no murder."

He repeats these phrases over and over, searing the false narrative into Grace's consciousness. As with the previous scene depriving Grace of her name, this moment does worse than ban Grace from asking journalistic questions. Instead, Emil *demands* those questions be asked, but only on his terms. Grace is not cut off or refused; rather, in Foucauldian fashion, she is opened up and coopted. She is a figure of what Herbert Marcuse calls "repressive desublimation," the aftermath of sixties countercultural expressiveness, now harnessed to authoritarian control.

At this point, with Grace drugged, inarticulate, lying prone in a madhouse, a feminist viewer might give up on *Sisters*. So far, Grace has served as our "strong female lead," but now she is rendered passive and helpless. But from my perspective, Grace's domestication is not a betrayal of feminism. It's rather a realistic depiction of women's prospects in a structurally patriarchal society. Grace has demonstrated every quality that could be desired from a tough, independent woman. Yet, she can't single-handedly escape her fetters. To achieve true freedom, she needs more than individual will; patriarchy itself must be abolished. For Grace's condition to be rendered in its full horror, the fantasy of the "strong female lead" must be undone.

Along these lines, David Greven makes the case that the dominant "positive images" argument—"The belief that representations of oppressed groups such as women, queers, and those of nonwhite races and ethnicities should cast these identities in an affirming light . . . has disturbingly blunted and distorted not only many works of art but a great deal of critical thinking."[135]

Greven suggests that some of the opprobrium leveled against Mulvey's once-central "Visual Pleasure and Narrative Cinema" essay emanates from this "positive images" position. The problem with Mulvey's formula, this critique goes, is that it doesn't account for the strength of will nor the active gaze of the oppressed. But as we will see, Grace's loss of agency isn't just a matter of disempowerment; her pacification under hypnosis links her to the repressed knowledge of a dead woman. Dominique was murdered by a medical establishment that saw her as a "freak" and so excluded her from the protected category of humanity. If Grace had simply fought back at this point, she might have been liberated, but Dominique's voice would go unheard.

With this critique of "positive images" in mind, Greven argues that the "post theory" turn in film studies may *seem* empowering, but in the end leads to an under-examination of gender, sexuality, race, and class. Greven sees De Palma as an example of the New Hollywood inheritance of Hitchcockian tropes that demand theoretical examination rather than to be taken at face value, as every representation of heterosexual masculinity in these films is also an estrangement. Since Greven's argument is central to my reading of *Sisters*, I'll quote it at some length:

> often the films deemed most problematic, even offensive; the representations that trigger the most controversy and condemnation; the directors whose off-screen reputations

> get read into their work in ways that make their work indefensible to many . . . make the boldest and most challenging statements about gendered identity. . . . The negative images—of women, queers, and other races . . . have very often been more revealing, urgent, poignant, and exciting than the concomitantly bland, anodyne, safe, 'progressive' image of oppressed identities.[136]

Sisters is not safe or tidy. The women in this film are "crazy." But we are still permitted glimpses of both Grace and Danielle's resourcefulness, charm, persistence, and resilience. Arguably, a truly positive feminism itself had become impossible by the time *Sisters* was made, since the widespread social rebellion that had inspired the movement was fading away. Accordingly, we see the waning of utopian culture and the rise of what Jon Greenaway calls "Gothic Marxism" as an aesthetics of resistance. This form is both critical and hopeful, rejecting "the positivist dogma of uncritical thought and the instrumentalist logic of capitalist realism, embracing the monstrous potential of a future that is still to be made."[137]

Chris Dumas credits De Palma with a sympathy to feminism "as he understood it in 1972 and 1973."[138] Dumas claims the director identified with feminism "precisely insofar as he could map his own loss onto its loss, his failure onto its failure—exactly because feminism was part of the 1960s . . ."[139] Feminism was a valuable "strand" in the radical movements to which De Palma felt committed. When these movements failed in realizing their radical vision, dissolving into single issues, they lost this collective horizon. Later, in his 2012 thriller *Passion*, De Palma will return to this impasse by exploring neoliberal, individualistic "empowerment," staging women who manipulate and murder each other in pursuit of opportunistic corporate success.

Nancy Fraser argues this detachment of women's rights from collectivity began when the feminist struggle for recognition began to dovetail "all too neatly with a rising neoliberalism that wanted nothing more than to repress all memory of social egalitarianism."[140] This severance of second wave feminism from its revolutionary origins led to an "uncanny doubling" where feminism became a dark mirror of itself. Politicized feminism looks in the mirror and is confronted with its girlboss doppelganger, "a strange shadowy version of itself, an uncanny double that it can neither simply embrace nor wholly disavow."[141] Positive representation of women in film tends to sanitize and simplify this problem, while in *Sisters* the twinning of feminist hope and despair reminds us of the work that still needs to be done and that historical context matters.

Fifty years later, Naomi Klein wrestles with this problem in her book *Doppelganger*, through which she explores her relationship to her dark twin, Naomi Wolf, a public figure whose similar appearance and profile to Klein's causes endless confusion among both women's fans and foes. Klein is mortified to be mistaken for her doppelganger, who was once a liberal feminist, and has now fallen prey to far right-wing conspiracy theories, becoming a talking head on the Steve Bannon/Joe Rogan circuit. This leads Klein to a fascination with the figure of the doppelganger as key to understanding our current political death drive. Klein becomes obsessed with this "ephemeral being that . . . represents the most repressed, depraved, and rejected parts of ourselves that we cannot bear to see—the evil twin, the shadow self, the anti-self, the Hyde to our Jekyll."[142]

In this swirling, vertiginous moment of *Sisters*, where Grace both is and is not herself, where she is cast into a shadow realm, where she is called upon to access the memories of what Jordan Peele might call the "tethered," where she is in danger of losing herself to fuse with this alter-verse, *Sisters* predicts the paranoid, postmodern doubling lamented by Fraser and Klein.

Sisters *directed by Brian de Palma*

Minute 72

In a classic study, Eve Sedgwick lays out the key indicators of the gothic mode—isolation and immobilization, live burial, sleeplike and deathlike states, doubling, the unspeakable—all of which are at play in *Sisters*.[143] Throughout the history of gothic fiction, these tropes have illuminated shadow selves that arise when women are forced to repress their needs and desires. In this moment, Grace will enter a deeper stage of the unconscious, leading her into this evocative gothic space.

Emil is not content to indoctrinate Grace with the message that "there was no murder." He follows this routine brainwashing by truly burying Grace alive, sending her into a deep hypnotic state where she will be forced to witness and experience Dominique's suffering and death. As she passes into this realm, Emil becomes Grace's whole world. His distorted face eclipses her vision, his echoing voice is the only sound she hears, he even directs her breathing. Twisting Grace's desire to uncover the facts, Emil wields this truth as punishment: "You came to watch us, to spy on us, to feed on our sorrows. . . . You want to know all our secrets? Fine. We will share them with you."

Minute 73

Sisters is not a body horror film except . . . The scar. Danielle and Dominique were conjoined twins. When they were separated, Danielle was left with a large, ridged scar on her outer thigh. We have seen the scar once before, when Danielle and Phillip were making love on the couch that will become his coffin. It was then shown as an ominous precursor to Phillip's murder. However, now, with more understanding of what Danielle has endured, we can see this scar as a trace of her former wholeness, connection, monstrosity, deviance, rebellion.

The fabric obscuring Danielle's scar is rent just as Grace enters a hypnotic dreamworld, suggesting that Grace is passing into Danielle's deepest trauma. The camera cuts jaggedly between Danielle's scar and extreme close-ups of Grace's alarmed eyes. We see Danielle on an adjacent bed with Emil leaning over her.

Danielle: Why is she here?
Emil (*very close to Danielle's face*): Don't you remember? She was always here. Don't you remember?

Fast zoom into Grace's eye. (A shot, says cinematographer Paul Hirsch, "beyond anything that had ever been technically before."[144]) This novum L-cut fills the screen with Grace's iris as Emil insists that Danielle, "Go back. Remember."

Through the looking glass we see Dr. Milius, shot grainily by a 16mm handheld camera. We have seen him before in the documentary shown at the *Life* office. But now we gaze through a reverse angle, from what we could call a "patient's eye view." The doctor, now dressed as a priest, repeats his analysis of the twins, but his voice uncannily echoes as if heard from a long, tunneled distance.

> **Milius:** I am in agreement with my colleagues. Although they believe that Dominique is the one who is truly disturbed, I think that they will find that Danielle, who is so sweet, so responsive, so normal, as opposed to her sister, can only be so because of her sister.

Dr. Milius's repeated pronouncement reminds us that Danielle is not the "good" sister but the "good" face of a complex whole whose entirety will never see the light of day. Now, at least, in the darkness, she is allowed a taboo, agential gaze at a camera that doesn't seem capable of looking back. It is not clear, however, if this witness is Grace, Danielle, Dominique, or all, or none.

Minute 74

The two sisters (Kidder and Salt) sit in a distorted, darkened theater, the parasitic Emil leaning over their chair. Nearby, young male triplets, dressed identically, tap dance in unison. A vertiginous camera wheels around the cavernous room, catching glances of other "freaks"—a little person, a man with a flipper-like arm, "Cathy the lobster child," "Eddie the giant"—surveilled by gawkers—"normal" people intruding on the girls with weaponized cameras.

In this expressionistic, black and white shadow realm, evocative of and influenced by *Rosemary's Baby*'s hallucinatory rape scene, Danielle will learn she is not the girl she imagines herself to be, but a monster. Robin Wood reminds us, however, that as enemies of the "normal," monsters are our film's heroes.

In this memory-scape Emil continues to exert hypnotic influence, urging Danielle to recall a picnic the twins attended when they were young, repeating the refrain "remember" again and again:

> **Danielle:** That's right the picnic. And the people have come to see us. They were my friends.
> **Emil:** They were your friends. . . . They brought their picnic lunches and their cameras. . . . And they brought their little children. . . . They gave you treats. . . . And then they asked whether they could take your picture. . . . Dominique didn't like the children very much.
> **Danielle** (*becoming more and more agitated through the rest of the conversation*): No, she said they were laughing at us.
> **Emil:** What did they call you?
> **Danielle:** I can't remember that.
> **Emil:** Try to remember what they called you.
> **Danielle:** I can't remember that.
> **Emil:** Remember!
> **Danielle:** They said, "freak." "Look at the freak."

This last word echoes insistently and hollowly.

Both Danielle and Grace are beautiful, "normal"-looking women. However, we must also see them as "monsters." Grace's threatening feminist independence and connection to leftist counterculture is linked to Danielle's former status as a conjoined twin, a "freak." Under Emil's hypnosis, this connection between the women is made literal, as Danielle is joined to Grace, who, in the psychedelic memory they inhabit, is now a substitute for or ghost-memory of Dominique.

What Linda Badley calls the "dreamlike mise-en-scène that externalizes [Danielle's] 'deep' psyche" is not just a revelation of Danielle's past, but an audacious flourish of cinematic inventiveness and technical mastery.[145] De Palma would rather chew his own arm off than toss out a wordy expository scene when allusive visual representation is an option. In an interview with Richard Rubinstein, he condemns the boring device of having a psychiatrist recount: "Remember when you were a little girl back at the institute . . . ."[146]

Instead of telling or showing the past, the director, in a long tracking shot, rolls out a Buñuelesque tapestry. This commitment to spectacle and technique is viewed by De Palma's fans and detractors alike as a kind of pure, cold formalism. To the contrary, De Palma's stylization here isn't simply objective visual "genius," but a moment where the film's themes are allusively conjured. In this transition to dream logic, "the self splits cinematically into different characters, and the performative nature of identity becomes visible," writes Badley.[147]

A self-proclaimed Brechtian, De Palma understands formal choices to be political. In denying the viewer straightforward "realism," he refuses to confirm our preconceptions of the world. Similarly, the ideally proportioned body and symmetrical features of a conventional film's protagonist operate ideologically, smoothing over the irregularities of real bodies as well as the contradictions of a society in which the individual is valued, argues John W. Meyer, "only under the condition that he become isomorphic, or similar in form, to all the other individuals in the society."[148] On the other hand, Danielle and Dominique's pre-op "extraordinary body," like De Palma's extraordinary cinema, upend the unspoken common sense behind "realism" and "normality."

In Minute 74, the film sides with excess, with freakishness, with the "abnormal." Conventional horror tropes, states Catherine Pugh, "constantly and consistently pit young, healthy, attractive characters against the hideously deformed and inherently evil."[149] However, *Sisters* subverts these tropes, showing Danielle, Dominique, and the other "freaks" on display to be cruelly stigmatized and victimized by "normates."

In an interview with Charles Highman, De Palma claims he *is* Grace at this moment, who herself has fused with Danielle/Dominique. His identification, he says, is further transmitted to the spectator: "The audience becomes this girl, peering through a psychological hole. Since, in a way, I am the girl, the people out there can be her too."[150] Notes David Greven, De Palma "exudes an ambivalence about—and a rivalrous identification with—his female characters rather than a misogynistic hatred."[151] This is what is so heartbreaking about his 1973 discussion at the American Film Institute. Listening, one witnesses the director's slow realization that he is faced with an almost all-white-male-straight (culturally as well as sexually) critical apparatus who can't imagine identifying with a "lady reporter" or a Black murder victim, let alone a conjoined twin.[152] Without the leftist, sixties countercultural "freaks" who nurtured De Palma's creative origins, imaginative solidarity becomes impossible.

According to Rosemarie Garland-Thompson, the "freak" is a site of liminality and confusion, blurring boundaries between human and inhuman. Once considered a marvel, a wonder, a religious mystery, in capitalist modernity she becomes a medical anomaly, a problem that must be clinically described and solved. She is a "magnet . . . to which culture secures its anxieties, questions, and needs at any given moment."[153] For this reason, we can't leave the "freak" alone. We must explain her, contain her, regulate her, surgically normalize her, pathologize her, silence her.

The figure of the "extraordinary body," Thompson argues, is not often analyzed in film and literary criticism, yet she is "essential to the cultural project of American self-making," a "figure[] of otherness that support[s] the privileged norm"[154] Her "natural" deviance conceals her body's overdetermination as a "legal, medical, political, cultural, and literary" construct crafted to shore up the normate's boundaries.[155] The surreal, Buñuel-esque dreamworld Grace enters when she returns to Dominique's "freak" origins makes sense in relation to this psychic excess generated by the notion of the "freak." As Jeffrey Jerome Cohen puts it, "the monster is the harbinger of category crisis"; she appears dangerous because she "threatens to smash distinctions" we rely on for a sense of selfhood.[156]

How does Danielle's status as sympathetic "freak" speak to *Sisters*' feminist themes? The film illustrates Garland-

Thomson's claim that we can't disentangle the categories of "freak" and "woman": "Both the female and the disabled body are cast as deviant and inferior; both are excluded from full participation in public as well as economic life; both are defined in opposition to a norm that is assumed to possess natural physical superiority."[157] The abjection of both women's and "freaks'" positions is underscored by their relation to each other: the disabled woman is a dark mirror of the "beautiful," objectifiable woman. Instead of attracting the male gaze, the former attracts the gaping "stare" discussed by Garland-Thomson: "The history of disabled people in the Western world is in part the history of being on display, of being visually conspicuous while politically and socially erased."[158]

For Garland-Thomson, disability and gender are analogous; both concepts pervade "all aspects of culture: its structuring institutions, social identities, cultural practices, political positions, historical communities, and the shared human experience of embodiment."[159] Femaleness and disability are similarly framed as "a natural state of corporeal inferiority, inadequacy, excess, or a stroke of misfortune."[160] Notes Alice Dreger, the attribution of "natural impairment" to women—"often couched as medical claims—were used to justify denying women the right to vote, to hold property, to make decisions about their own bodies."[161]

The kinship between sexism and ableism goes back to Aristotle, who saw women as "mutilated males." And then there is the well-worn presentation of women as castrated, lesser versions of men. Intersex people and "bearded ladies" become "freaks" simply by exhibiting both masculine and feminine attributes.[162] Garland-Thomson reminds us that conjoined twins share with intersex people a reputed threat to the "natural" order of things—with conjoined twins contradicting "our notion of the individual as discrete and autonomous . . .." and intersexed infants challenging "our insistence that biological gender is unequivocally binary."[163] For intersexed people this leads doctors to routinely perform non-consensual operations on infants, while instructing parents to forever conceal these children's variations from them. It's only with the intersex movement, Juliana Gleeson argues, that the resultant trauma has come to light.[164]

Yet, because conjoined twins and intersex people threaten normality, they also offer possibility. Christopher Breu speculates intersexuality's transgressions have visionary potential—"indexing what is possible to build and sustain where a collective sense of queerness as solidarity, desire, and embodiment is produced . . . .."[165] Relatedly, Elizabeth Grosz suggests that intersexual people challenge sexual polarity, offering the possibility that "sexed subjects could be seen to occupy a position within a sexual continuum."[166]

Yet, the utopian horizons of flying one's "freak flag high" are generally ignored, and instead these corporeal and gendered outliers are held up to discipline "normates," who fortify their own social inclusion by maintaining elaborate borders between themselves and "the other." Ironically, Garland-Thomson notes, disciplining the body to be ideally feminine can itself lead to disability, as in the impacts of the nineteenth-century corset.[167] We can look at Danielle's forced severance from her sister in this light. This normalizing procedure did not lead to her liberation, but rather triggered a mental illness that drove her to unconsciously murder her only ally.

In her book on conjoined twins, *One of Us*, Alice Dreger introduces a term for the horrific procedure Danielle and Dominique were forced to undergo—"sacrifice surgery," a procedure that kills one twin to save the other. This is, says Dreger, "the only case in which surgeons are given explicit permission to separate a brain-live person . . . from the organs keeping her alive, so that someone else may survive."[168] Somehow, this conjoined twin is not "one of us," not a person with the same right to live as every other (singleton) individual. In one horror-like detail of a sacrifice surgery, we learn

> Just before the operation, nurses painted Angela's fingernails pink, in an effort to prevent the surgeons from being

> confused about which "half" was to be salvaged: they were to save the girl with the pink fingernails.[169]

Dreger is shocked by the lack of ethical outcry against sacrifice surgery and supposes that, tacitly, doctors and decision-makers are adopting the

> "monster approach"—an approach based on the assumption that conjoined twins are so grotesque that they are not really human. Therefore, we are justified in doing anything medically reasonable to make at least one of them "human," even if it will very likely result in both of their deaths.[170]

Especially in the United States, the values of individualism and independence won't allow for the interdependence of conjoined twins. Says Dreger, "the biographies and autobiographies of conjoined twins reveal that the limits on these people's freedom stem chiefly not from their conjoinment per se but from the thoughts and actions of others."[171] In many cases where children are operated on, "the doctor doesn't really believe that the social system is broken; it's the child that's broken."[172] Any child or adult who insists on embracing her "broken," "extraordinary body," Garland-Thomson concludes, will thus be subject to the normate's enthralled and repulsed "stare."

In Minute 74 we witness this stare. Danielle and Dominique once imagined they were guests at a picnic. They were simply "normal," cute children enjoying a day out. But now, in this moment of Freudian *Nachträglichkeit* (afterwardness or retrospective knowledge), Danielle realizes she and her sister were not guests at the picnic, but rather spectacles at a freak show. The adults who gave them treats were less caretakers than tourists on safari to the exotic land of "Siamese" twins, there to "shoot" their prey with flashing, weaponized cameras. Says Garland-Thomson, "If the male gaze makes the normative female a sexual spectacle, then the stare sculpts the disabled subject into a grotesque spectacle. The stare is the gaze intensified, framing her body as an icon of deviance."[173] As half of a conjoined twin, Danielle is her own doppelganger who has experienced the male gaze as a woman beautiful enough to earn her living as a model (and to be sexually harassed by a photographer as she mentions during her date with Phillip), as well as the crowd's stare as a "freak" whose proportions and lack of individuality are unimaginable to the "normate" voyeur.

Kier-La Janisse points out that throughout this film the "'aloneness' of people is emphasized in order to elevate the bond between twins."[174] This suggests that, as rebels from the normal, conjoined twins are figures of social fantasy. Their "anarchic" bodies exhibit "a potential for individual freedom denied by cultural pressures toward standardization," as Garland-Thomson says of freak show performers.[175] This supports Cohen's sixth thesis, "Fear of the monster is really a kind of desire."[176]

Naomi Klein points to this utopian horizon of twinning in the final chapter of her political memoir of life as a kind of doppelganger. Despite her enmity for her evil twin—ex-feminist, current-conspiracy-theorist Naomi Wolf—she learns to embrace one aspect of her twinned experience. As she "loses" her identity, she comes to question our societal overvaluation of individualism itself. Doppelgangers are a wildly popular cultural trope, not just because we fear our uncanny others but because they bear a message impossible to say straightforwardly in "capitalism's hall of mirrors"—separation and illusions of sovereignty are not our only options, we can strive toward "interconnection and enmeshment."[177] The conjoined twin's membership in a repressed bestiary "haunts the capitalist imagination." If we listen closely, Jon Greenaway hints, these figures "whisper [] to us that the world does not have to be this way."[178]

As conjoined twins, then, Danielle and Dominique's attachment is not only "enfreakment" but also collaboration. At the picnic, Danielle shields Dominique from the cameras' flashes, comforting her sister while the "normal" onlookers take cruel pleasure in the freakishness of children. For Danielle and Dominique, as for Klein, doubling is a potential model of intimacy, a message that "connections and solidarities and kinships are available to all of us should we choose to guard the boundaries of our selves less jealously."[179]

Minute 75

"Freak. Freak. Freak." The words echo as another seemingly generic bourgeois woman approaches the twins for a snapshot. But this time, it's Grace's mother who appears behind the apparatus. "Sweetie smile," she insists, full of venomous treacle. Grace's face registers horror in reaction to her blithely callous mother while Danielle's desperate, disembodied voice begs, "Make them go away from me, please."

This is the big reveal—Danielle's "primal scene" is a repressed memory that she was once called a "freak." De Palma's identification with Danielle here is palpable. "Freak" is an umbrella term for the ragtag coalition of weirdos that comprised the sixties' counterculture giving form to the director's personality and aesthetic. If mainstream media and political leaders called them "freaks," the term was quickly and gleefully appropriated by the counterculture itself. Danielle's tragedy is not that she *was* a "freak," but that she lacked a collective of fellow "freaks" with whom to bash back. As the sixties waned, De Palma, too, feels this contraction of his world.

An iris-wipe-out through Grace's enlarged eye and we are back to the asylum where Emil prepares the women for another harrowing stroll down memory lane. This shuttling back and forth from the Canadian Loisel sanatorium for "freaks" and the unnamed asylum for "crazy" people in Staten Island implicitly compares the two institutions' cruelty while illuminating something both Bill Finley (Emil) and De Palma often say in interviews. To the common-sense notion that Emil is the villain of *Sisters*, they respond that he is a red herring, indicating that the film's true antagonist lies elsewhere.

In a 2004 interview, Finley notes his character is named after the surrealist writer Andre Breton, which makes perfect sense in this moment where he serves as a warped master of ceremonial dreams.[180] In fact, there is no plot-related reason for Emil to compel Grace to "remember" Danielle's trauma. Rather, ambiance eclipses narrative. And, not accidentally, this is the moment where we truly confront "the other" in the film, not as our enemy, but as the force that is "oppressed and repressed," as Wood says.

Emil leans smotheringly close to Danielle's face, compelling her to "remember . . . what you learned last spring that you could never have." Danielle resists, but Emil pushes on, reminding her that because she was a freak, she "could have no home, no husband, no children, no baby." In short, she couldn't be a woman in the ways that count. She relents, "Yes, I remember that."

And once more we are shuttled through Grace's tremulous eye to a hallucinogenic dreamscape depicting Danielle's past traumas. Cut to a scene of Emil and Danielle embracing on a gauzy white bed. We view them through an iris lens shot that is theatrical while connoting surveillance, akin to earlier shots through binocular lenses. The camera moves to reveal Dominique lying next to the lovers, miserable, disrupting their intimacy. When the camera returns to Danielle, she has detached from Emil's arms. Scolding, she tells Dominique: "You're supposed to be sleeping." And then, as Emil strokes her face, the final betrayal: "Why can't you make her go away? Can you make her go away? Please. Please." Emphasizing this scene's classic feminist implications, Barbara Creed analyzes this memory as "a bizarre primal scene in which woman is depicted as a 'double' figure, only capable of sex if her twin selves are split from each other. The man is the aggressor who deliberately silences woman's critical self in order to appeal to her 'desire' to be a wife and mother."[181]

Minute 76

Emil pulls away from Danielle to get something out of his medical bag as the camera zooms back from its iris frame to reveal another level of voyeuristic complicity. A couple of shadowy figures watch the scene through a two-way mirror—Creed reads this as Grace's projection of herself as a journalistic spectator, doubling her role as object and subject of the gaze.[182] Emil pulls out a large needle and plunges it into Grace. In a moment of great pathos, Grace/Dominique begs: "Help me. Don't hurt me. Don't hurt me." None of the four onlookers intervene. Instead, the observers behind the mirror take notes as the camera zooms in on Emil and Danielle kissing passionately. Dominique is excluded from the shot, as she will soon be excised from Danielle's body and from the world of the living.

Minute 77

Zoom out via Grace's tortured eye. Now we are back in the asylum. Emil's insectile form leans claustrophobically over Danielle's supine figure, leeching her traumatic memories. In a trance, Danielle compliantly recollects a time when she and her sister walked through the sanatorium's garden and Danielle confessed to being pregnant. To understate, Dominique reacted poorly. Rather than respond to Danielle's professed hope that the sisters could share the baby when it was born, Dominique killed the fetus with a pair of garden shears (adding significance to our glimpse of this tool in a previous scene). We watch Danielle closely, through a warped, fisheye lens as she relives the pain of losing her baby, and now, as then, is certain she is going to die.

Unlike the rest of Danielle's memories shown in this section of *Sisters*, the forced abortion is not a visual flashback, but retold by Danielle in the present. Since De Palma has professed commitment to the "show not tell" method of exposition, I initially wondered if *Sisters*' budget simply wouldn't allow for another dramatic set piece, and then had my suspicion confirmed when listening to a 1973 discussion with the American Film Institute.[183] De Palma needn't have worried. Margot Kidder's talent transports us into Danielle's struggle with and against this traumatic memory.

No doubt, Bill Finley and others who worked on *Sisters* attribute the power of Kidder's performance to the actor's real-life misery on the set. Finley, editor Paul Hirsch, and others have remarked in interviews that Kidder, who was dating De Palma while making the film, had frequent outbursts and crises on set. Yet, assuming an organic connection between an actress's real-life feelings and her emotional expression on camera follows a misogynist trend in the (mostly male-authored) assessments of actors' interpretations of their characters. In these accounts, men's outstanding performances are seen as marks of talent and rigor, while women's performances of similar quality are thought to be unconscious, natural outgrowths of their emotional states. When a male performer draws on his experience, he's "method acting," while a woman is a kind of hysteric.

In fact, directors have historically used this stereotype as an excuse to abuse actresses. The most horrific example is perhaps *Last Tango in Paris*, where director Bernardo Bertolucci conspired with Marlon Brando to rape Maria Schneider with a stick of butter to elicit the reaction they sought, rather than trust she could do her job. This practice of tormenting women actors to evoke an "authentic" response is not always so dramatically sinister, but it is cruelly common, as in *Possession* and *The Shining* where directors pushed their actresses to the brink of sanity to heighten their performances.

De Palma is not innocent of this practice. Some instances are mild and perhaps even generative, as when he casts real mothers and daughters to play mothers and daughters in *Sisters* (Jennifer Salt and Mary Davenport) and *Carrie* (Amy Irving and Priscilla Pointer). But, while making *Carrie*, he also forced Betty Buckley (playing Coach Collins) to use private information she had to taunt Amy Irving (playing Sue) to intensify Irving's performance. Further, De Palma compelled Buckley to genuinely "whack" Nancy Allen (playing Chris) rather than perform a staged hit. Even more sadistically, he made the actors repeat the scene again and again, urging Buckley to "hit her harder" each time, resulting in the latter actress's genuine pain and bruising.[184] Says Allen, who later married De Palma, he "wanted a particular reaction and for some reason didn't trust that he could just tell me that."[185]

Against these belittling tendencies, I submit that Kidder's performance in this demanding role is emotionally controlled and intellectually rigorous. Here, at a moment where she must relive her deepest trauma, she is terrified, confused, dazed, and intense. As is appropriate for the moment, she is neither naturalistic nor comically gonzo. In other scenes she must make subtle choices about how to appear flirtatious, humorous, psychotically murderous, closed-off, disheveled, compassionate, cagey, and guilty, all while maintaining a consistent French Québécois accent. Each choice she makes feels true to her character and interestingly specific.

Kidder's performance is another reminder that *Sisters* is not simply the ingenious artistic accomplishment of a singular brilliant mind but a product of an ensemble that includes creative women making unique choices in writing the script and representing their characters. Kidder brought to the role of Danielle a background of literary interest, counterculture credentials, and struggles with gender-related trials. These conditions don't simply "naturally" bleed into her performance, as some might claim, but they do inform her work.

Kidder grew up in a small city in Northern Canada, where she early on became politicized while struggling with mental health issues, for which, throughout her life, she would be periodically publicly humiliated. She always wanted to be an actress, but faced challenges such as suffering through an illegal abortion performed by injecting Lysol into her uterus. After relocating to the United States, she became a popular

TV actress and moved into a beach house with Jennifer Salt. Not only did Kidder meet and fall in love with De Palma during this phase of her life, but she and Salt transformed their home into a salon and party pad attracting the who's who of Hollywood's counterculture.

The most popular document highlighting this scene is Peter Biskind's book, *Easy Riders, Raging Bulls*, which narrates the rise of New Hollywood as a uniquely director-centric artistic movement—"This was to be a directors' decade if ever there was one. Directors as a group enjoyed more power, prestige, and wealth than they ever had before."[186] Directors of previous eras were much more controlled by the studio system, often regarding themselves as "hired help." New Hollywood directors were freer to conceive of themselves as great artists, with unique defining styles.[187] Of course, Biskind includes De Palma among this elite group. However, Kidder's and Salt's narration figures centrally in the book. Clearly these women, though "mere" actors, were central to the scene's sensibility.

It was Salt who decided to move to Hollywood, galvanizing De Palma to follow.[188] Salt met Kidder at an audition, and that friendship cemented much of the New Hollywood scene when they moved into their $400 a month "lopsided A frame" at Nicholas Beach, with a tie-dyed flag flying in front. The house was "unfashionably far from the action," but became a "magnet for young Hollywood" as more of the New Hollywood scene moved into the area.[189]

Kidder and Salt were clearly ambitious young people with strong opinions, artistic aspirations, and dreams themselves, but were also expected to fulfill all the scene's required "womanly duties"—offering sex, procuring drugs, preparing meals, and planning parties. Salt, who should have been as free as male counterparts to hone her craft and enjoy her life, found her mind perpetually crowded with plans to please the men around her:

> I was always thinking, Should it be chili and the three bean salad and the cheesecake or should we barbeque chicken....

> I cooked for these boys, gave lots of parties, made them take drugs and take their pants off and get down.[190]

Kidder theorized the roles she and Salt took on:

> The reality was that we always got the drugs and we always got the food and we basically served our guys, the whole time putting down the notion that we as women would do that. There was a real contradiction in what we perceived ourselves to be doing and what in fact we were doing.[191]

Biskind relies on Kidder's narration to describe the rise of New Hollywood, but also uses patronizing language to describe her as a "tramp" bad girl who "was sexually aggressive, not to say ravenous, slept with nearly every man who crossed the threshold."[192] He goes on to label her an unstable drug addict, contra her own claim that she used drugs for mind expansion and self-exploration.

Kidder's analyses of the scene are some of the most interesting in the book, and it's also notable that the fluidity and the experimentalism of the times allowed her, a working-class woman, to break into a scene comprised mostly of upper-class artists (such as De Palma and Salt). In this ferment, De Palma, with the help of Louisa Rose, wrote *Sisters* as a vehicle for Salt and Kidder (at least that's the story written in *Easy Riders, Raging Bulls* and often repeated—other sources claim De Palma hoped to cast Marlo Thomas, a bigger star, in the role of Grace). The dynamics between De Palma and Kidder are not fully known, but on-record male commentary concentrates on Kidder's volatility, rather than De Palma's cold detachment, both of which were elements in the mix, as Jennifer Salt notes in an interview.[193]

Unlike many of that generation's Hollywood creatives who became centrist liberals or conservatives as the political tides changed, Kidder only grew more radical through the years up until her death at age seventy by suicide. In the early 1990s, she was branded "Baghdad Betty" for questioning the Gulf

War. She outspokenly contested fracking and was arrested for protesting the Keystone Pipeline in 2011. Shortly before she died, she supported socialist presidential candidate Bernie Sanders and protested the Dakota Access Pipeline at Standing Rock. In fact, the ill health that may have contributed to her suicide stemmed from her endurance of freezing temperatures during these protests.

Kidder also wrote scathing critical screeds for left-wing magazines like *The Nation* and *CounterPunch*, often targeting the Democratic Party for its betrayals of leftist ideals. In an article lambasting her home state's right-leaning Democratic senator, Max Baucus, she complained, "America's centre has been tap dancing to the right since Ronald Reagan was loosed upon the world and it hasn't taken a backwards step yet."[194] (She fortunately didn't have to see where we landed in 2025 as I write this book.)

True to the themes of gendered oppression and madness in *Sisters*, Kidder's struggles with mental health can't be extracted from her political disappointments. As she said in the same article for *CounterPunch*:

> Sadly, the hard truth is that it's hard not to feel like a little baggie of leftover peas in the face of the seeming omnipotence of these corporations, these dictates from above. Inertia and depression are logical responses to such an enormous monolith of corruption.

In 2016, Kidder wrote a piece about trying to enjoy the natural beauty surrounding her but getting distracted by

> the visions of all the dead children in Syria that Hillary Clinton helped to kill; the children bombed to bits in Afghanistan and Pakistan from Obama's drones, the grisly chaos of Libya, the utter wasteland of Iraq, the death and destruction everywhere caused by American military intervention.[195]

At this point, she was embarrassed to live in the United States:

> The Ukraine, Honduras, El Salvador, Guatemala, Chile, you name it—your country has bombed it or destroyed its civilian life in some basic way. And there you all are tonight, glued to your TVs and your computers, your hearts swelled with pride because you belong to the strongest country on Earth, cheering on your Murderer President. Ignorant of the entire world's repulsion. You kill and you kill and you kill, and still you remain proud.[196]

In light of this righteous tirade, Kidder's Canadian standpoint (that she shares with her character, Danielle) is significant. This outsider status gives her critical purchase on US bellicosity.

In *Sisters*, Kidder's character Danielle is overwhelmed by these kinds of authoritarian antagonists—a conformist society that calls her a "freak," a doctor/husband who has whittled her down to her "acceptable" femininity, carceral institutions whose nurturing facades hide chambers of cruelty and murder. The passion Kidder later pours into protesting injustice contributes to the experience of *Sisters* as a full-blooded horror film rather than the cold, formal, "clinically detached" exercise De Palma's films are sometimes derided as, and could, perhaps, become, if fully controlled by one great auteur.[197]

Minute 78

A final zoom through Grace's eye. Then an iris wipe into an operating theater, seemingly sprung from the thigh of a grainily shot Buñuel film. Danielle and Dominique/Grace are laid out on an operating table erected in the swimming pool seen in the documentary, *Blanchion Twins Separated*. The "twins" are surrounded by a voyeuristic crowd consisting of priests, a pair of male hippie twins, nuns, young female patients draped in hospital gowns, the journalist from *Life*. Once again Emil, now wearing hospital scrubs, hovers possessively over

Danielle and Dominique/Grace. He commands, "do not be afraid . . . I am a surgeon, you have lost your baby, you are bleeding very badly. The only way I can save you is to separate you from Dominique."

Danielle retreats from Emil's forceful narration, into her smallest, most feminine, passive voice. She asks, "Am I going to die?" Emil answers, "No, *you* will be fine," insinuating that Grace/Dominique—or Danielle's active, angry half—will *not* be fine. He commands Danielle to "sleep, sleep, sleep." Dramatic music plays as a heavily gloved hand reaches under water and into a box of cutlery, reminiscent of Danielle's cursed prize from the gameshow *Peeping Toms*. A close-up on that hand slowly raising a giant cleaver. As it goes with dream logic, this hand belongs to the P.I., Larch, Grace's ally and nemesis. He stares at the blade intently with a small cruel smile.

This climactic staging in an operating theater points to centuries of "cures" aimed at crushing women's bodies and spirits. The surgical amputation of Dominique from Danielle has nothing to do with healing, and everything to do with control. Going into the surgery, Emil knows Dominique will die. That sacrifice, though, is the point. Danielle will become a "normal," conventionally beautiful woman whom he can marry and who will bear his children, while her rebellious noncompliance, embodied by Dominique, will be snuffed out.

This surgical travesty points to the more general ways the female body itself has been, from capitalism's inception, a thing to be tamed, transformed, ratiocinated, and medically manipulated. This "object" must not only be refashioned to emphasize its fertility, its sexual appeal, and its passive smallness in comparison to the male body, it must also be conditioned to renounce joy and desire, accommodating itself to labor. Like burning a witch, separating conjoined twins is aimed at eliminating all that is deviant, deindividualizing, and excessive. It's a transformation, suggests Silvia Federici, of "the individual and social body into a set of predictable and controllable mechanisms."[198] This violence recreates woman as a creature "capable of regular, homogenous and uniform behavior, indelibly marked with the memory of the new [gender binaristic] roles," argues Federici. The wonder, magic, and uniqueness of the "freak" is sacrificed to produce a standardized, conforming body.[199]

Federici describes this rationalistic world view eclipsing pre-capitalist modes of life as one where humans divorced themselves from corporality and nature, exchanging solidarity for king-like mastery of mind over slavish body.[200] This Cartesian self-domination where one "confront[s] one's body as an alien reality" subordinated to capitalist work discipline, is the model for larger power structures, such as the state over the social body.[201] With this, medical institutions, such as the Loisel institute, became a means to discipline the body in "an attempt by state and church to transform the individual's powers into labor power."[202]

Federici compares this division to a "true vivisection of the human body, whereby it was decided which of its properties could live and which, instead, had to die."[203] Women's bodies were analogous to natural resources that needed to be parceled: "Like the land, the body had to be cultivated and first of all broken up, so that it could relinquish its hidden treasures."[204] In the end the goal was to kill the body, insofar as the body served as a form of pleasure—"The body had to die so that labor-power could live."[205]

With this sacrifice "the concept of the body as a receptacle of magical powers that had prevailed in the medieval world" was also murdered.[206] The "irrational" body was criminalized so that the "mechanical body" could prevail, a transition that could not be enforced "without the destruction by the state of a vast range of pre-capitalist beliefs, practices, and social subjects whose existence contradicted the regularization of corporeal behavior . . .."[207] This is the framework through which Federici reads the attack on witchcraft, but she could just as well be discussing the destruction of "freaks" or those with extraordinary bodies, such as conjoined twins, who once were seen as magic and powerful beings, and now stood as useless and terrifying medical anomalies.

"Freaks," then, are not welcome in the world Danielle and Dominique were born into. *Sisters*, however, condemns Dominique's amputation. In fact, Dominique, in a sense, survives her murder to wreak her revenge, possessing Danielle who will finally castrate and murder her sister's killer. In this, *Sisters* continues the tradition of Tod Browning's *Freaks* in which physically anomalous circus performers bond together to gain retribution against a world that ridicules and vilifies them.

Minute 79

The cleaver is passed reverently, ritualistically, from one (twinned) observer to the next—priests, hipsters, nuns. In the background, the *Life* writer sits flanked by two look-alike patients in hospital garb who could double for Manson girls. Finally, Emil, dressed in surgeon's garb, receives the surgical instrument/sacrificial implement/weapon, raising it ceremoniously. A brief shot of Grace's terrified face. A dramatic pause and Emil brings down the cleaver. Cut to Grace, back in the asylum, screaming.

Emil shakes her by the shoulders, commanding her to "relax, relax." In the adjacent bed, Danielle babbles, "I'm sure you've come back, Dominique. . . . Please come back." But Emil reminds her, repeatedly, "Dominique is dead."

I think the scene is suitably surrealistically creepy, but it's not what De Palma wanted. The film's editor Paul Hirsch notes:

> In the last section of the dream, the cinematographer overexposed the film. Brian was very upset—it had all those extras from the circus, holding candles, and they had been sent back home; so, Brian came up with a different concept for the scene, and included Charles Durning and the reporter from *Life* magazine.[208]

While the intended presence of "freaks" would have driven home the film's condemnation of "othering," the final version's twins and religious figures have their own resonance. Notes Mary Poovey in her account of the "ideological work of gender" in medical practices, religion has systematically been used to erase midwives and other women from the field of obstetrics and other female-specific medical practices, to "consolidate [the] social authority" of male doctors. This patriarchal travesty is evoked in *Sisters*' comically reverent ceremony conducted by zanily costumed authority figures including doctors and priests.[209]

Minute 80

Cards on the table, I find Minutes 80 and 81 to be throwaways. Here, De Palma violates his own rules and over-explains what he has already shown. A close-up of Emil's lips against Danielle's ear as he itemizes (at too much length) that Dominique is dead, that he wants Danielle to accept Dominique's death, that he wants to marry her, that they had trouble making a new start because Danielle couldn't forget Dominique, that "sometimes you even became her to reassure yourself of her existence."

We know all this. Why does De Palma tell us? Is he losing faith in cinema's ability to convey more than words alone can? Are we seeing a slide into the commercialism that will drag down some of his future efforts? My questions were answered when I found an interview in which De Palma admitted these moments were the casualty of his scant budget.[210] To be fair, the scene does reinforce the important theme that Danielle was coerced into passive femininity. And, of course, we are awash in Emil's endless reservoir of creepiness as we build to his satisfying demise.

Minute 81

The scene drags on as Emil continues murmuring in Danielle's ear. In this moment, at least, we learn something new. Emil explains that the trigger for Danielle's transformation into

Dominique is sex. But this is not (just) because Dominique is repressed or moralistic, it is because all sex reminds her of Danielle's sex with Emil, Dominique's murderer. When Dominique killed Phillip, in her mind, she was killing her executioner. Says Emil to Danielle, "To Dominique, any man that made love to you is me."

Now, perhaps, Emil exhibits a death wish, or at least his lust overpowers his survival instinct. Massaging Danielle's breast, he conjures her dead sister. What could go wrong?

Here, we are reminded of the classic 1942 Jacques Tourneur/Val Lewton horror film *Cat People*, where (Kidder look-alike) Irena is triggered by sex to transform into a killer panther, attacking boring heterosexuals and would-be rapist psychoanalysts alike. In *Sisters*, as in *Cat People*, the monster is, of course, the heroine—"the most sympathetic character and emotional center," says Wood of Grace/Danielle/Dominique.[211] Yet, Wood follows with the caveat that these monsters can't "be conceived in positive terms." If Danielle and Dominique are on some level heroines, they have also "been perverted, turned destructive, by the length and thoroughness of the repression."[212]

Minute 82

Maybe Emil sees himself as an exorcist, purging his docile mate of her defiant alter-ego. But his psychiatric and medical expertise are no match for Danielle's repressed rage. All along he has been leaning over her like a demon about to smother its prey. Now, as he bends down for the kiss, a jump cut to his slithery mouth convinces us that he will suck the life out of Danielle.

But it's no longer Danielle below his lecherous mouth. It's Dominique, squinting through confused, unfocused eyes, pushing him away. She scurries around the room, attacking him with his own instruments of repression—hurling bottles of pills in his direction. He backs her against the sterile white wall, between a roll of white paper towels and a white doctor's coat, as the music slowly and eerily intensifies, run through

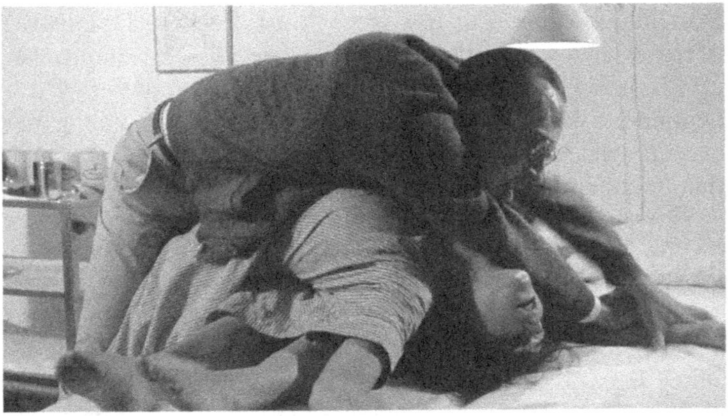

Sisters *directed by Brian de Palma © American International Pictures 1972.*

with a tremulously alien synthesizer. He pulls the bloody murder weapon from his doctor's bag. Like scalpels and pills, this is a tool to discipline and punish his wife/ward. Forcing her to look at the knife, he insists that she "remember" Phillip's murder, at once exorcizing Dominique and asserting Danielle's vulnerability and guilt.

Minute 83

Danielle remembers the cake Phillip brought her, remembers making a wish, remembers blowing out candles. But even as she submits to Emil's pop-Freudian methods, recounting the events she had previously repressed, her hand has other ideas. It creeps toward a medical tray. Her fingers close around the scalpel Emil may have used to tear her from her sister. With perfect symmetry, just as she confesses to cutting Phillip, she slashes Emil, castrating and murdering him at once, unleashing Herrmann's screeching strings.

Luridly red, viscous blood spurts from Emil's crotch. As Danielle tries to run from the body, Emil grasps her around the waist. She drags her burden to the table where Grace lies, still passed out. Emil twists Danielle around so that she falls backward over Grace in the position of the woman in Henry Fuseli's 1871 oil painting, *The Nightmare*. Emil inhabits the position of the incubus crouching over this figure in the painting but Danielle has slashed the impish look right off his face. And perhaps Grace, who lies slightly off-center from the spectacle, and whose eyes have been portals to an unearthly dreamworld, is the painting's "night mare" itself, the nearly invisible horse whose glowing, pupil-less eyes bear witness to the unholy couple.

Says Robin Wood, "Sisters is concerned single mindedly with castration; the symbolic castration of the woman within patriarchy, the answering literal castration that is the form of her revenge."[213] Castration includes, as Wood broadens its definition, man's impulse "to destroy the active aspect in order to construct the feminine woman who will accept her subordination."[214] With the resolution we have just witnessed—Dominique castrating Emil—Wood sees *Sisters* as a nearly perfect film: "the monstrousness of woman's oppression under patriarchy, and its appalling consequences have never been rendered more vividly."[215]

In psychoanalytic framings of castration, Freud's concept of the "Law of the Father" is key. To avoid castration, the child must enter the patriarchal symbolic order (patriarchal values, language, culture) and renounce his desire for unity with the abjected maternal/feminine, which he now recognizes as castrated. But we can reverse this formula and see Emil's castration as liberation, an escape from the harsh requirements of masculine discipline. In this sense, Emil becomes another "twin" of Danielle, Dominique, and Grace as his body is piled on theirs, his hand entwines with Danielle's. Says Laurent Bouzereau: "for a moment, they look like they're all conjoined, triplets, bound by blood."[216]

Perhaps Emil's merging with Danielle and Grace supports Carol Clover's notion that male horror audiences identify across gender with the final girl. But the reversals deepen

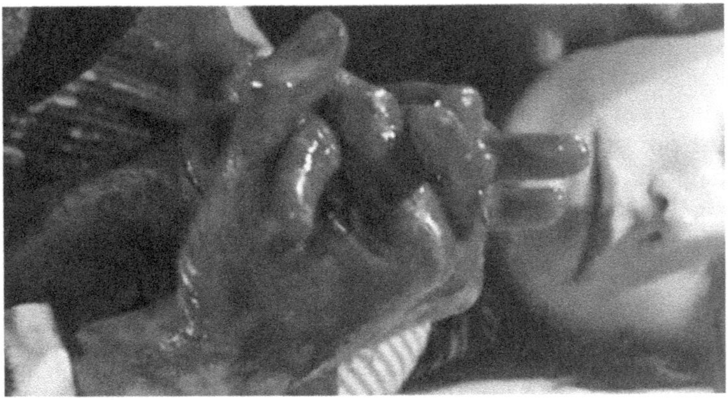

Sisters *directed by Brian de Palma*

when we engage with Barbara Creed's discussion of *Sisters* and castration in her classic book, *The Monstrous-Feminine*. The slasher film, she argues, addresses castration anxiety by "representing women in the twin roles of castrated and castrator," a process literalized in *Sisters*.[217]

Analyses of *Sisters*, Creed argues, recognize Danielle as a "castrated woman," but ignore her flip side as Dominique, the "femme casatrice." Creed is conflicted about De Palma's stance toward this figure—"On the one hand, the film sets out to terrify the spectator with an image of woman as psychotic castrator. On the other hand, it presents an interesting explanation of woman's oppression within patriarchy."[218] To me, this ambivalence seems consonant with De Palma's reflexivity. He's not going to deny his fear (as a typical heterosexual male) of sexually aggressive women, but he *is* going to thematize this fear.

Minute 84

If this were a film about a "strong female lead" this would be Grace's moment of triumph. Not only has she "solved"

Phillip's murder case, she has also uncovered the true cause of Dominique's death, an achievement beyond even illustrious *Life* magazine reporters. But, predictably, this victory will be Pyrrhic.

With Danielle and Emil piled on top of her, Grace slowly awakens from her trance. The world appears irreal. She prods Emil's inert body to be sure it exists. Slowly, orienting to her reality, she realizes she's buried under a dead man. Her hyperventilation erupts into a scream that becomes the wail of an ambulance's siren as we cut to the next scene.

Minute 85

More irresolution follows as the medics remove Emil's corpse from the asylum. Danielle, affectless, follows the body out. She is confronted by Detective Kelly, the thick-bodied, thick-headed cop who first searched her apartment.

> **Kelly:** Are you prepared to confess to the murder of your husband Emil Breton?
> **Danielle:** I have never hurt anyone in my life.
> **Kelly:** You claim you have a sister who did it?
> **Danielle:** My sister died last spring.

Danielle has accepted her sister's death, but we're left with confusion. Is Danielle admitting guilt? To what extent does she believe Dominique is real? If neither she nor her sister are responsible for Emil's death, who is? We never find out. This—one of the film's three "endings," according to Bouzereau—is unsatisfying, but perhaps that's the point.[219] In other films where a "crazy" woman finally confronts her crimes, the audience anticipates closure. Here, we are left where we began, to grapple with uncertainty, with structural violence that can't be attributed to any individual "criminal," and with our own complicity. Danielle alone gets closure, the worst kind. She's going to jail, probably for life.

Minute 86

Grace, a husk of the woman we knew, emerges from the asylum, propped up by her parents.

Cut to a new scene. Detective Spinetti drinks coffee and reads a newspaper, leaning casually against his car in front of a large suburban house dappled with sun flares. The camera tilts up, pushing voyeuristically toward a bedroom window.

Grace is back home, but not her own, adult home—the one decorated with posters of Angela Davis. Instead she's in her parents' house, in her childhood room, surrounded by dolls and pin-ups of cute male celebrities. She's a Stepford girl, changed out of her hip housedress and vinyl jacket and into a fuzzy white nightgown. Instead of smoking cigarettes, she eats candy.

Like this, Grace is infantilized, regressed, sitting pliantly before Detective Kelly whom she once so bravely confronted. She smiles at him, thanks him, offers him chocolates. Her mother attends her bedside as if Grace were a helpless little girl. Now that Detective Kelly knows Danielle is a murderer he is forced to believe Grace's story, but for Grace and for Phillip, it's too late.

Sisters *directed by Brian de Palma*

Minute 87

Grace's memories, along with her agency, have been erased. She can only regurgitate the words fed to her by a dead man: "It was all a ridiculous mistake. There was no body." This sentence triggers the camera to slowly pan in a 180-degree arc. We see that the back of Mrs. Collier's head has been obscuring a large Raggedy Ann doll sitting next to Grace, placed in a parallel position. Now that Grace has been turned into a traditionally feminine, doll-like automaton, she is twinned with yet another "sister."

On the wall are old-fashioned high school yearbook pictures of herself alongside teen idols from the fifties and early sixties. It's not just that the politicized late sixties, symbolized by the Angela Davis poster in Grace's apartment, are over, it's as if they never happened. Grace's denial goes beyond Phillip's murder; Emil's hypnosis has eradicated her historical memory altogether. To Detective Kelly, she repeats the hollow phrase: "you're making a ridiculous mistake . . . there was no body, because there was no murder."

Echoing Emil's former incantation, Detective Kelly pressures Grace to "remember." When Grace first reported Phillip's murder, Kelly implied she was imagining it under the spell of female hysteria. Now, he insinuates, it's her hysteria that leads her to deny the crime. She can't win but neither can he. Kelly's cajoling is fruitless. He quickly becomes resentful toward this disobedient female—"What else do you want me to do? Apologize in print? I sent you candy!"

Offscreen, the men of *Sisters* have been busy gossiping about Grace. Detective Kelly has called her editor/lover who has told him about Larch, the bullying PI she briefly worked with. But though these patriarchal forces are closing in on her, as the camera's slow circular pan has come to represent, she is beyond reach. Anyway, if she did manage to "remember" that Danielle killed Phillip, what would be the result? It would only add to Danielle's persecution rather than get at the root causes for Phillip's murder. Maybe, paradoxically, Grace's amnesia is the film's final gesture at refusal.

If we project forward to a later De Palma film, the Raggedy Ann doll gains significance. *Carrie* also features this doll, appearing in "final girl" Sue's room during that film's coda. In both cases, perhaps, the demonic doll signifies that the "tamed" woman's dark doppelganger still lingers. Says Douglas Keesey, "The bleeding hand will haunt until we recognize it as our own."[220]

Grace's final "catatonic state of guilt and impotence" characterizes the resolution for many of De Palma's protagonists. These endings, though, are not signs of the director's nihilism. Rather, these defeated characters are embodiments of post-Sixties disappointed hope—"the assassinations, the conspiracies, and the ever-encroaching media, with its unyielding message of conformity and materialism."[221] De Palma was always going to be a filmmaker, but this vocation had come to feel like an impotent afterthought in the face of media cooptation that made his talk of revolution "just another piece of software [the media] could sell, like aspirin or deodorant."[222]

This revolutionary mourning, I submit, calls for critique rather than the celebration of "strong female leads" or anything else. Thus, the irresolution of *Sisters*' last minutes is darkly appropriate.

Minute 88

Having failed to coax Grace into compliance, Detective Kelly now threatens her: "If there wasn't a body, why did you make such an accusation? You know how serious that could be?"

Whereas pre-asylum Grace would never have let her mother speak for her, now she cedes the floor. Mrs. Collier insists, "Grace has never deliberately told a lie in her life. You have to understand that she's not quite herself."

This phrase is a stealth bomb, bringing the theme of doubling back to center stage. If Grace is not herself, who is she? Visually, she's positioned in a line-up of her previous selves. To her right hang three portraits from her teen years. Their wildly varied styles emblematize rapid-fire cultural shifts that have formed the backdrop of her young life. To her left we see Grace as an anonymous child in her class pictures from elementary school. In the foreground sits her bourgeois mother, a potential future version of Grace. Positioned amid all these selves, harried by Detective Kelly, Grace becomes increasingly disturbed, furious that her truth will never be acknowledged, but impotent to articulate this message.

I submit that this, Grace's final moment onscreen, is powerful despite its anticlimactic dejection. Her show of impotent fury amid her many selves serves as a cinematic condensation of the individual's vulnerability before systemic forces. Grace is not a "strong female lead," but rather a woman created and dismantled by history and circumstance. She is a lesson in empathy and strategy. The urgent task isn't to fight for the triumph of our singular, indomitable heroines, but rather against the traumatic conditions impacting *all* women and men—Grace, Danielle, Dominique, even Emil.

Abigail Coykendall echoes this cri de coeur in her examination of Carrie's final flaming defeat. Carrie's "abjected, repressed, feminine traits" are more than characterization, but rather represent a general sense of disenfranchisement.[223] Like Grace, Carrie is less a "strong female lead" than a damaged monster produced by a world that "was already profoundly destroyed by an underlying thematics of cultural genocide, the fascism inherent in everyday American life."[224]

In sum, Grace's journey from outspoken feminist to infantilized child is not, as some have read it, a satire of feminism or a misogynist fantasy, but a tragedy in which the audience moves from detached voyeur to Grace's sympathetic "twin."

In this vein, Robin Wood argues De Palma's ambivalent identification with his women characters adds significance to his films' feminism. These women are not only repressed because they are women, they also represent a man's compulsion to repress his masculinity in order to construct himself as a "socially correct man . . . of patriarchy."[225] The anxiety surrounding De Palma's woman characters can be traced to the director's "identification with the 'feminine' and the inevitable dread that such identification brings with it."[226]

Minute 89

Grace utters the final spoken line in the film: "I'm fine! There's absolutely nothing wrong with me. All I know is there was no body because there was no murder." Following this closing denial, the scene dissolves to superimpose Grace onto a cow (yes, you read correctly). The cow stands adjacent to a rural Canadian train station, next to bags of onions as well as Phillip's coffin-couch "straightjacketed in its white moving blankets" as Marc Olivier—minutely attentive to the film's sofa imagery—notes.[227]

The camera slowly zooms out from a high angle medium shot to reveal a tractor puttering toward the scene. A farmer emerges from the vehicle and drags the cow away in what we can interpret as a reprise of Grace's subjugation. As the camera pulls further back, we see detective Larch strapped to a telephone pole, disguised as a repairman, looking at the scene through binoculars. He has followed the sofa to this "foreign" land in hopes of finding colluders with the murderers. However, though the story of Phillip's murder and sequestration is complex, we are not in *that* kind of conspiracy—the kind that can be solved.

Larch's comically rotund body suspended high in the air is all the closure we get, and perhaps deserve. This irresolution, however, creates an opening in a genre that often conforms to what Fredric Jameson calls a "reifying structure" that "consume[s] . . . the rest of the narrative."[228] Says Carrie

Rickey, *Sisters*' open-ended finale depicting Larch peering through binoculars yet seeing nothing of import, tells us, finally, looking reveals "only the what, not the why."[229]

Those who have had the temerity to watch the 2006 remake of *Sisters* learn little from it, but the remake's reliability and banality do help us understand that the original film has the bones of a perfectly conventional horror flick. The later version closes by showing Danielle (here called Angelique) and Grace (still called Grace) pacing the garden of a madhouse in terrifying symmetry. After being hypnotized by the film's Emil equivalent (named, gloriously, Dr. Philip Lacan), Grace ends her days permanently lost in the consciousness of the dead twin, Dominique (or here Annabelle). Many such banally generic conclusions exist for *Sisters*. De Palma's shaggy ending, though, refuses to give us closure and instead goes rogue.

This last moment's tonally jarring surrealism seems closer to *Greetings* and *Hi, Mom!'s* counterculture picaresque than to *Dressed to Kill* or *Blow Out's* narrative coherence. In this moment we depart from expected tropes. Observes Badley, "the perpetrator, the body, and the white male protagonist—are all missing." Instead, we are met with "savage postmodern irony."[230]

Sisters' final implied thesis matches that of Joshua Gooch's book on the horror genre, "Capitalism Hates You." Rather than therapy, catharsis, or relief, critical viewers look for horror that "give[s] form to the negative feelings that imbue our historical moment."[231] The misguided detective/voyeur, Larch, will remain on his uncomfortable stakeout for hours or for days. For the viewer, though, this is "THE END" as the words appear over this strange, disjunctive scene. Fade to black.

NOTES

Preface

1 Forrester, C., "When De Palma Became De Palma," *Establishing Shot*, September 18, 2023. Available online: https://blogs.iu.edu/establishingshot/2023/09/18/when-de-palma-became-de-palma/.

2 Wood, R., "An Introduction to the American Horror Film," in B. K. Grant (ed.), *Robin Wood on the Horror Film: Collected Essays and Reviews* (Wayne State University Press, 2018), 80.

3 Dumas, C., *Un-American Psycho: Brian De Palma and the Political Invisible* (Intellect, 2012), 26.

4 Wood, "An Introduction," 102.

5 Ibid.

6 Ibid., 79.

7 Wood, R., "*Sisters*," in B. K. Grant (ed.), *Robin Wood on the Horror Film: Collected Essays and Reviews* (Wayne State University Press, 2018), 139.

8 Wood, R., "Brian De Palma," in B. K. Grant (ed.), *Robin Wood on the Horror Film: Collected Essays and Reviews* (Wayne State University Press, 2018), 370.

9 Tarantino, Q., *Cinema Speculation* (Harper, 2020), 191; Olivier, M., *Household Horror: Cinematic Fear and the Secret Life of Everyday Objects* (Indiana University Press, 2020).

10 Fraser, N., "Feminism, Capitalism and the Cunning of History," *New Left Review* 56 (2009): np. Available online: https://newleftreview.org/issues/ii56/articles/nancy-fraser-feminism-capitalism-and-the-cunning-of-history.

Minutes 1–88

1 De Palma, B., "Murder by Moog: Scoring the Chill," *Sisters* Blu-ray pamphlet (Criterion, 2018), 29. (Original essay *Village Voice*, October 11, 1973.)

2 Rubinstein, R., "The Making of Sisters: An Interview with Brian De Palma," in L. Knapp (ed.), *Brian De Palma: Interviews* (University Press of Mississippi, 2003), 5.

3 Smith, S., *A Heart at Fire's Center: The Life and Music of Bernard Herrmann* (University of California Press, 2002), 321.

4 De Palma, "Murder by Moog," 31.

5 Coykendall, A., "Bodies Cinematic, Bodies Politic: The 'Male' Gaze and the 'Female' Gothic in De Palma's Carrie," *Journal of Narrative Theory* 3, no. 30 (2000): 333.

6 Mulvey, L., "Visual Pleasure and Narrative Cinema," in L. Mulvey (ed.), *Visual and Other Pleasures* (Palgrave Macmillan, 2009), 15.

7 Dumas, *Un-American Psycho*, 25.

8 Ibid.

9 Ibid.

10 Wood, "Brian De Palma," 369.

11 Greven, D., *Psycho-Sexual: Male Desire in Hitchcock, De Palma, Scorsese, and Friedkin* (University of Texas Press, 2013), 207.

12 Tarantino, *Cinema Speculation*, 178.

13 Dumas, *Un-American Psycho*, 31.

14 Coykendall, "Bodies Cinematic," 344.

15 MacKinnon, K., *Misogyny in the Movies: The De Palma Question* (University of Delaware Press, 1990), 187.

16 Dumas, *Un-American Psycho*, 169.

17 Coykendall, "Bodies Cinematic," 334.

18 Dumas, *Un-American Psycho*, 89.

19 Coykendall, "Bodies Cinematic," 335.

20 Hilsabeck, B., "Double Vision: Global Irony in Brian De Palma's *Sisters*," *New Review of Film and Television Studies* 3, no. 22 (2022): 724; 723.

21 MacKinnon, *Misogyny*, 63.

22 Badley, L., "De Palma's Embattled Red Period: Hitchcock, Gender, Genre, and Postmodernism," in D. Lennard (ed.), *The Other Hollywood Renaissance* (Edinburgh University Press, 2020), 106.

23 Davis, A., "Rape, Racism and the Myth of the Black Rapist," in A. Davis (ed.), *Women, Race, and Class* (Vintage, 1983), 173.

24 White, A., "The Fine Art of Cruising: What makes De Palma's *Dressed to Kill* a Gay Movie Landmark," *Out Magazine*, September 9, 2015. Available online: https://www.out.com/armond-white/2015/9/09/what-makes-de-palmas-dressed-kill-gay-movie-landmark#:~:text=Due%20to%20De%20Palma's%20comic,expectations%20and%20gender%20categories%2C%20too.

25 Greven, *Psycho-Sexual*, 245.

26 Badley, "De Palma's Embattled," 106.

27 Pally, M., "Double Trouble," in L. Knapp (ed.), *Brian De Palma: Interviews* (University Press of Mississippi, 2003), 93.

28 Ibid., 94.

29 Kidder, M., "My Fellow Americans: We Are Fools," *Counterpunch*, July 29, 2016. Available online: https://www.counterpunch.org/2016/07/29/my-fellow-americans-we-are-fools/.

30 Childs, M. and Jones, A., "De Palma has the Power!" in L. Knapp (ed.), *Brian De Palma: Interviews* (University Press of Mississippi, 2003), 40.

31 Badley, "De Palma's Embattled," 105.

32 Williams, L., "Film Bodies: Gender, Genre, and Excess," *Film Quarterly* 4, no. 44 (1991), 4.

33 Déborah, Z. and Herzog Dessites, D., "The Autopsy," Criterion, 2004.

34 Ashbrook, J., *Brian De Palma* (Pocket Essentials, 2000), 33.

35 Klein, N., *Doppelganger: A Trip into the Mirror World* (Farrar, Straus and Giroux, 2023), 56.

36 Cole, J., "Brian De Palma Sisters," *Not Just Movies*, 2010. Available online: https://armchairc.blogspot.com/2010/06/brian-de-palma-sisters.html.

37 Bouzereau, L., *The De Palma Decade* (Running Press Adult, 2024), 19.

38 "Audio from a 1973 discussion with De Palma at the American Film Institute," Blu-ray special features, Criterion, 2018.

39 Smith, *A Heart*, 323.

40 Ibid.

41 Ashbrook, *Brian De Palma*, 10.

42 Appelbaum, R., "Techniques of the Horror Film," in L. Knapp (ed.), *Brian De Palma: Interviews* (University Press of Mississippi, 2003), 63.

43 Rubinstein, "The Making," 10.

44 Greven, D., *Representations of Femininity in American Genre Cinema: The Woman's Film, Film Noir, and Modern Horror* (Palgrave MacMillan, 2011), 93; Williams, T., "Re-working Hitchcock: Brian De Palma's *Sisters* (Criterion Collection)," *filmint.*, November 2018. Available online: https://filmint.nu/hitchcock-criterion-collection/.

45 Rickey, C., "Psycho-Thriller Qu'est-ce Que C'est," Pamphlet Criterion Blu-ray, 2018, 9.

46 Rubinstein, "Interview with Brian De Palma," Pamphlet Criterion Blu-ray, 19.

47 Brecht, B., "Alienation Effects in Chinese Acting," in J. Willett (ed.), *Brecht on Theater* (Radha Krishna, 1957), 92.

48 Keesey, D., *Brian De Palma's Split Screen: A Life in Film* (University Press of Mississippi, 2015), 61.

49 Ashbrook, *Brian De Palma*, 11.

50 Badley, "De Palma's Embattled," 106.

51 Knapp, L., "Introduction," in L. Knapp (ed.), *Brian De Palma: Interviews* (University Press of Mississippi, 2003), xiv.

52 Quoted in ibid.

53 Wood, R. "*Sisters*," in B. K. Grant (ed.), *Robin Wood on the Horror Film: Collected Essays and Reviews* (Wayne State University Press, 2018), 139.

54 Keesey, *De Palma's Split Screen*, 62.

55 Greven, *Psycho-Sexual*, 124.

56 Bartholomew, D., "De Palma of the Paradise," in L. Knapp (ed.), *Brian De Palma: Interviews* (University Press of Mississippi, 2003), 25.

57 Tarantino, *Cinema Speculation*, 183.

58 Greven, *Psycho-Sexual*, 126.

59 Ibid., 143.

60 Ibid.

61 Davis, *Women, Race*, 177.

62 Greven, *Psycho-Sexual*, 143.

63 Wood, "Brian De Palma," 370.

64 Dumas, *Un-American Psycho*, 164.

65 Knapp, "Introduction," xiii.

66 Brecht, "Alienation Effects," 92.

67 Bouzereau, *The De Palma Decade*, 20–1.

68 Olivier, *Household Horror*, 95.

69 Ibid., 96.

70 Greven, D., "The Most Dangerous Game: Failed Male Friendship in De Palma's Snake Eyes," *CineAction*, Winter, 2022: 55.

71 Greven, *Psycho-Sexual*, 123.

72 Badley, "De Palma's Embattled," 111.

73 Ibid., 110.

74 Man, G., "Apparatus, Genre, and Spectatorship in the Classroom," *Educational Perspectives* 42, no. 1–2 (2009): 17.

75 Bordwell, D., *The Poetics of Cinema* (Routledge, 2008), 59; Man, "Apparatus," 18.

76 Mulvey, "Visual Pleasure," 17.

77 Silverman, K., *The Subject of Semiotics* (Oxford University Press, 1983).

78 Ibid., 201.

79 Ibid., 201–2.

80 Quoted in ibid., 215.

81 Ibid., 223.

82 Ibid., 232.

83 Ibid.

84 Mulvey, "Visual Pleasure," 26.

85 Olivier, *Household Horror*, 11; 23.

86 Knipfel, J., "An Interview with Screenwriter Louisa Rose," *The Chiseler*, 2019. Available online: https://thechiseler.org/home/an-interview-with-screenwriter-louisa-rose.

87 American Film Institute Discussion, Criterion Blu-ray.

88 Knipfel, "An Interview with Screenwriter Louisa Rose."

89 Álvarez Lopez, C. and Martin, A., "De Palma, Pure and Unpure," *Film Critic: Adrian Martin*, 2018. Available online: https://www.adrianmartinfilmcritic.com/essays/depalma.html.

90 Jacobs, K., "How the World's Largest Landfill became New York's Biggest New Park," *Curbed New York*, September 2016. Available online: https://ny.curbed.com/2016/9/13/12891320/freshkills-park-nyc-staten-island-engineering-design.

91 "Fresh Kills: The Inside Story of the Recovery Operation after 9/11," *9/11 Memorial & Museum*, 2023. Available online: https://www.911memorial.org/events/fresh-kills-inside-story-recovery-operation-after-911.

92 "New Interview with actor Jennifer Salt," Criterion Blu-ray *Sister*, 2018.

93 Bouzereau, *De Palma Decade*, 15.

94 Wood, "*Sisters*," 135.

95 Ibid.

96 Badley, "De Palma's Embattled," 103.

97 Ibid., 109.

98 Tarantino, *Cinema Speculation*, 195.

99 Ibid.

100 Vicino, M., "*Sisters* Review," *Letterboxd*, 2020. Available online: https://letterboxd.com/brat/film/sisters/.

101 Badley, "De Palma's Embattled," 103.

102 Quoted in ibid., 113.

103 Ibid.

104 Quoted in ibid., 104.

105 Dumas, *Un-American Psycho*, 174.

106 Ibid., 172.

107 Ibid., 24.

108 Tarantino, *Cinema Speculations*, 184.

109 Dumas, *Un-American Psycho*, 157.

110 Quoted in Badley, "De Palma's Embattled," 112–13.

111 Dumas, *Un-American Psycho*, 165.

112 Tarantino, *Cinema Speculations*, 190.

113 Ibid.

114 Jameson, F., "Periodizing the 60s," *Social Text* 9/10 (1984): 208.

115 Dumas, *Un-American Psycho*, 114.

116 Benjamin, W., 'On the Concept of History," in H. Eiland and M. Jennings (eds.), *Selected Writings, 4* (Harvard University Press, 1940), 390.

117 Jameson, F., "Cognitive Mapping," in C. Nelson and L. Grossberg (eds.), *Marxism and the Interpretation of Culture* (University of Illinois Press, 1988), 349.

118 Ruda, F., "Always Jamesonize!" *E-flux Notes*, October 2024. Available online: https://www.e-flux.com/notes/633672/always-jamesonize.

119 Cohen, J., "Monster Culture (Seven Theses)," in J. Weinstock (ed.), *The Monster Theory Reader* (University of Minnesota Press, 2020), 41.

120 Bouzereau, *De Palma Decade*, 21.

121 Coykendall, "Bodies Cinematic," 332–3.

122 Ibid., 333.

123 Sobczynski, P., "It Was All a Ridiculous Mistake!: Brian De Palma's Sisters Hits Blu-Ray," *RogerEbert.com*, October 2018. Available online https://www.rogerebert.com/streaming/it-was-all-a-ridiculous-mistake-brian-de-palmas-sisters-hits-blu-ray.

124 Freud, S., *The Uncanny*, trans. D. McClintock (Penguin, 2003), 132.

125 Olivier, *Household Horror*, 47.

126 Ibid.

127 Silverman, K., *The Acoustic Mirror: The Female Voice in Psychoanalysis and Cinema* (Indiana University Press, 1988), 72.

128 Ibid., 75.

129 Olivier, *Household Horror*, 63.

130 Clover, C., *Men Women and Chainsaws: Gender in the Modern Horror Film* (Princeton University Press, 2015), 30–1.

131 Olivier, *Household Horror*, 106–7.

132 Wood, *American Nightmare*, 100.

133 Gilman, S., "The Image of the Hysteric," in S. Gilman, H. King, R. Porter, G. S. Rousseau, and E. Showalter (eds.), *Hysteria Beyond Freud* (University of California Press, 1993), 298.

134 Ibid., 306.

135 Greven, *Psycho-Sexual*, 8.

136 Ibid., 13.

137 Greenaway, J., *Capitalism: A Horror Story: Gothic Marxism and the Dark Side of the Radical Imagination* (Repeater, 2024), 180.

138 Dumas, *Un-American Psycho*, 234.

139 Ibid., 234–5.

140 Fraser, "Feminism, Capitalism," np.

141 Ibid.

142 Klein, *Doppelganger*, 8.

143 Kosofsky Sedgwick, E., *The Coherence of Gothic Conventions* (Routledge, 1986).

144 Bouzereau, *De Palma Decade*, 23.

145 Badley, "De Palma's Embattled," 111.

146 Rubinstein, "The Making," 6.

147 Badley, "De Palma's Embattled," 111.

148 Quoted in Garland-Thomson, R., *Extraordinary Bodies* (Columbia University Press, 2017), 68.

149 Pugh, C., "Beautiful Monsters: Sickness, Disability and the Extraordinary Body," *Studies in Gothic Fiction* 6, no. 1 (2018): 54.

150 Quoted in Keesey, *De Palma's Split Screen*, 86.

151 Greven, *Psycho-Sexual*, 123.

152 American Film Institute Discussion, Criterion Blu-ray.

153 Garland-Thomson, R., *Freakery: Cultural Spectacles of the Extraordinary Body* (NYU Press, 1996), 2.

154 Garland-Thomson, *Extraordinary Bodies*, 5.

155 Ibid., 6; 8.

156 Cohen, "Monster Culture," 40.

157 Garland-Thomson, *Extraordinary Bodies*, 19.

158 Garland-Thomson, R., "Staring at the Other," *Disability Studies Quarterly* 25, no. 4 (2005): 56.

159 Garland-Thomson, R., "Integrating Disability, Transforming Feminist Theory," in C. McCann, S. Kim, and E. Ergun (eds.), *Feminist Theory Reader* (Routledge, 2020), 336.

160 Ibid.

161 Dreger, A., *One of Us* (Harvard University Press, 2004), 149.

162 Garland-Thomson, "Integrating Disability," 338.

163 Ibid., 341.

164 Gleeson, J., *Hermaphrodite Logic: A History of Intersex Liberation* (Verso, 2025), 1.

165 Breu, C., *In Defense of Sex: Nonbinary Embodiment and Desire* (Fordham University Press, 2024), xi.

166 Grosz, E., "Intolerable Ambiguity: Freaks as/at Limit," in J. Weinstock (ed.), *The Monster Theory Reader* (University of Minnesota Press, 2020), 279.

167 Garland-Thomson, "Integrating Disability," 340.

168 Dreger, *One of Us*, 8.

169 Ibid., 88.

170 Ibid., 93.

171 Ibid., 48.

172 Ibid., 72.

173 Garland-Thomson, "Staring at the Other," 26.

174 Janisse, K., *House of Psychotic Women* (FAB Press Ltd., 2012), 85.

175 Garland-Thomson, *Extraordinary Bodies*, 68.

176 Cohen, "Monster Culture," 49.

177 Klein, *Doppelganger*, 326.

178 Greenaway, *Capitalism*, 178.

179 Ibid., 325.

180 Criterion Blu-ray, "Bill Finley Interview."

181 Creed, B., *The Monstrous-Feminine: Film, Feminism, Psychoanalysis* (Routledge, 1993), 133.

182 Ibid.

183 Criterion Blu-ray, AFI interview.

184 Keesey, *De Palma's Split Screen*, 123.

185 Ibid., 124.

186 Biskind, P., *Easy Riders Raging Bulls: How the Sex-Drugs-and-Rock'N'Roll Generation Saved Hollywood* (Simon & Schuster, 1999), 15.

187 Ibid.

188 Ibid., 151.

189 Ibid., 231.

190 Ibid., 232.

191 Ibid.

192 Ibid., 231.

193 Criterion Blu-ray, Interview with Jennifer Salt.

194 Kidder, M., "Ax Max," *CounterPunch*, December 7, 2009. Available online: https://www.counterpunch.org/2009/12/07/ax-max/.

195 Kidder, "My Fellow Americans."

196 Ibid.

197 Dumas, *Un-American Psycho*, 81.

198 Federici, S., *Caliban and the Witch: Women, the Body and Primitive Accumulation* (Autonomedia, 2004), 244.

199 Ibid., 146.

200 Ibid., 148.

201 Ibid., 152.

202 Ibid., 133.

203 Ibid., 140.

204 Ibid., 140–1.

205 Ibid., 141.

206 Ibid.

207 Ibid.

208 Bouzereau, *De Palma Decade*, 23.

209 Poovey, M., *Uneven Developments: The Ideological Work of Gender in Mid-Victorian England* (University of Chicago Press, 2009), 50.

210 Criterion Blu-ray, AFI interview.

211 Wood, "*Sisters*," 135.

212 Wood, "World of Gods and Monsters: The Films of Larry Cohen," in B. K. Grant (ed.), *Robin Wood on the Horror Film: Collected Essays and Reviews* (Wayne State University Press, 2018), 141.

213 Wood, "Brian De Palma," 370.

214 Ibid.

215 Ibid.

216 Bouzereau, *De Palma Decade*, 23.

217 Creed, *Monstrous-Feminine*, 127.

218 Ibid., 136.

219 Bouzereau, *De Palma Decade*, 24.

220 Keesey, *De Palma's Split Screen*, 104.

221 Knapp, "Introduction," xiv.

222 Quoted in ibid.

223 Coykendall, "Bodies Cinematic," 350.

224 Ibid., 352.

225 Wood, "Brian De Palma," 369.

226 Ibid., 370.

227 Olivier, *Household Horror*, 107.

228 Jameson, F., "Reification and Utopia in Mass Culture," *Social Text* 1 (1979): 132.

229 Rickey, "Psycho-Thriller," 12.

230 Badley, "De Palma's Embattled," 107.

231 Gooch, J., *Capitalism Hates You* (University of Minnesota Press, 2025), 2.

INDEX